D1422764

BETH AXFORD

is a writer, digital marketer and *Doctor Who* enthusiast.

She has written for publications such as the *Radio Times*, *Digital Spy*, the *I*, *New Statesman* and the official *Doctor Who* website. Beth created The Time Ladies, a *Doctor Who* blog, podcast and YouTube channel. She has also featured in *Doctor Who* magazine and hosted panels at Comic-Con.

Beth currently works in marketing and as a freelance writer, and can be found on Twitter and Instagram @0hMySt4rs.

THE
DOCTOR
WHO
QUIZ BOOK

Travel the Whoniverse and test your
knowledge in the ultimate quiz

BETH AXFORD

First published in the UK by John Blake
An imprint of Bonnier Books UK
4th Floor, Victoria House,
Bloomsbury Square,
London, WC1B 4DA

Owned by Bonnier Books
Sveavägen 56, Stockholm, Sweden

Hardback ISBN – 978-1-789-466-67-6

A CIP catalogue of this book is available from the British Library.

Designed by Envy Design Ltd
Printed and bound in Great Britain by Clays Ltd, Elcograf S.p.A.

3 5 7 9 10 8 6 4 2

Copyright © Beth Axford, 2022

Wordsearches on pages 60-61 and 138-139 courtesy of www.thewordsearch.com
Internal illustrations © Shutterstock

John Blake is an imprint of Bonnier Books UK
www.bonnierbooks.co.uk

CONTENTS

INTRODUCTION

As this book hits your shelves, *Doctor Who* is almost sixty years old and has a viewership of millions of people across the globe. Thousands of us over the years have fallen in love with the Doctor and the TARDIS, whose doors have opened up the world for us when we jump aboard.

So, what brought you to *Doctor Who?* Some of you might have stumbled upon it in its early years, when there were fewer TV channels to choose from and *Doctor Who* and its wobbly sets were a staple of family television. Others may have had the baton passed down by parents, eager to introduce you to the Doctor and their friends. Some of you, like me, may have discovered the show when it returned in 2005 after nearly 16 years off-air, when the TARDIS grabbed hold of the hearts of a whole new generation.

My story is unlike most of the other fans I've encountered. I happened to stumble upon a *Doctor Who* sticker book in early 2006 on my way home from school. I think it must have been Billie Piper that stuck out to me! I'd caught a glimpse of the show during the Ninth Doctor's regeneration the year before, and distinctly remembered this working-class, blonde woman who saved the world. Her story reminded me of my own life growing up in a council house, and she gave me hope. I persuaded my mother to buy me the sticker book, of course. I took it home, read it from cover to cover and sat down for the newest episode of the show as it aired the following Saturday. It featured Sarah Jane Smith, a beloved classic *Who* companion, who helped the Doctor and his friends save the Earth from a bunch of nasty Krillitanes.

I was hooked.

The show has been a huge part of my life ever since. I grew up with the Tenth Doctor and survived my teenage years with the Eleventh. I entered young adulthood in confusion with the Twelfth Doctor and realised who I wanted to be with the Thirteenth. I went back and escaped with the First Doctor when things got too tough. With each incarnation I felt supported and it is funny how perfectly they fitted with the different stages of my life. The Doctor is not only a hero but a friend, and an introduction to the most wonderful universe.

I like to think that *Doctor Who* makes the best of us. The show helps us to learn and causes us to question. It inspires creativity and community through a shared passion, and helps us to turn away from our shadows and come into the light when we might have been feeling lost.

For many, the show symbolises escapism and hope. The community it has created for its fans alone is beautiful, spanning the entire world and thousands of people who might otherwise never have crossed paths. One of the best and most important themes is chosen family, which has trickled down into the group of people who have chosen loved ones through celebrating all that *Doctor Who* is. It has also been widely celebrated for its portrayal of a non-violent hero and well-rounded female characters, as well as forays into progression and representation.

There's something for everyone aboard the TARDIS. You might find yourself relating to a companion or character that makes you feel seen and helps you to move through the world more authentically. Some fans and viewers just love exploring faraway worlds and meeting scary villains. Others might find the show educational, which was the original intention of the producers, way back in 1963. That is the beauty of a show so rich in history, that can go anywhere throughout space and time; we get to explore ourselves and the world around us without ever leaving our sofas.

For us fans, *Doctor Who* can be a lifestyle rather than just a TV show. We don't just watch the TARDIS materialise on our screens, we read the books, listen to the audios and create our own *Doctor Who* adventures through art, writing or media. There's an ever-growing list of ways you can explore the Whoniverse and be a fan. No matter how much you've watched, or how you celebrate the show, *Doctor Who* is for you, and so is this book.

These pages serve as a celebration of everything we love about our beloved hero and their universe: the characters, the adventures, the villains and the lessons! There are three sections: easy, medium and hard, split across fifteen chapters, so you'll be able to find all of your favourites here, where there really will be something for everyone.

For most questions in this book, I'm referring exclusively to adventures or characters within the television show canon. This is to make things accessible and clear; after all, not everybody has seen every episode, listened to every audio or read every comic! However, in some places, I will cover the extended Whoniverse such as television and audio spin-offs – and in these places I will directly refer to or mention an adventure or character from outside of the main show.

I think, above all, that *Doctor Who* is about inclusion and bringing hope to the world. At the heart of the show is the notion that everybody is worthy, no matter who they are. That everyone is important, no matter where you come from. That's what keeps us watching and adventuring through space and time, holding onto that hope that we belong. This book is a celebration of that. I hope that you feel included within these pages – and that you know there is always a place for you aboard the TARDIS with the Doctor.

Chapter One

THE DOCTOR'S MANY FACES

Over the past six decades, the Doctor's face has changed over a dozen times. From a white-haired man in a junkyard to a mysterious blonde woman in a rainbow shirt, the Doctor has saved the universe with many personalities and an equal number of outrageous outfits. Armed with a sonic screwdriver, a time machine and a clever brain, the Doctor has shown us countless times that kindness, bravery and using our minds can be the most powerful way to change the world.

For many, the character has been a hero and a force for change, taking up residence in our televisions and our hearts. Each incarnation has inspired a new generation, battling aliens and saving the day with their wits and a dash of charm. The Doctor is one of those characters that can be so relatable, yet so far away. They are alien, yes, but feel and think as we do, wanting to spread peace wherever they go.

Perhaps it is their persistence and imperfections that we have fallen in love with. Their willingness to always try to do the right thing and sometimes get it wrong. Maybe we just love their humour, warmth and the adventures they take us on. From the Thirteenth Doctor and her hopeful speeches to the Fourth Doctor and his endearing jokes, there's something special woven through the hearts of each and every Doctor.

Everyone has their favourite. You might have grown up on long scarves and Jelly Babies or a pinstriped suit and Converse. Some of us have several favourites or a Doctor we're itching to see more of. Whichever Doctor you're drawn to, they will always be the renegade Time Lord we've come to know and love, ready to grab our hand and take us on an adventure.

You might have watched every Doctor regenerate. Or maybe you've been too heartbroken to move on from your favourite. However many Doctors you've adventured with, there's always something for everyone. A new friend to get to know.

We've laughed and cried as they've shown us the wonders of the universe. We've hidden behind our sofas when they've faced off against a deadly Dalek or a creepy Cyberman. We've faced dreamscapes and nightmares and have even been inspired. The Doctor in their TARDIS, travelling the stars and helping out; and we've run with them, all the way.

So, how well do you know the many faces of the Doctor? In this chapter, you'll find a host of Time Lord questions, celebrating every regeneration of our two-hearted hero.

1. *Doctor Who* began in November 1963. Which actor played the very first incarnation of the Doctor, debuting in the first episode, 'An Unearthly Child'?

A) Matt Smith

B) William Hartnell

C) Peter Cushing

2. Patrick Troughton took over as the Second Doctor in 1966. Which instrument did this Doctor play regularly to 'help him think'?

A) A guitar

B) A recorder

C) A violin

3. When Jon Pertwee took over the role and became the Third Doctor in 1970, the character had been exiled to one planet as a result of violating the Time Lords' non-interference policy. Which planet was the Doctor sent to?

A) Mars

B) Saturn

C) Earth

A Way to Keep the Doctor on Our Screens

Regeneration was first introduced to *Doctor Who* in 1966 when the producers needed a way to continue the show after William Hartnell was no longer able to play the Doctor. They came up with the idea that the Doctor could renew their face and body when sick, injured or decaying, resulting in Patrick Troughton taking over the role. However, the term 'regeneration' wasn't used on-screen until the Doctor's third regeneration in 'Planet of the Spiders' (1974)!

4. True or False? Tom Baker was cast as the Fourth Doctor after Jon Pertwee's departure in 1974. As of publication, Baker is currently the longest-serving Doctor.

5. The Fifth Doctor, played by Peter Davison, included a vegetable in his outfit that he claimed would turn purple in the presence of toxic gases. Which vegetable did he wear on his lapel?

A) Celery

B) Broccoli

C) Carrot

6. Which actor played the rainbow outfit-wearing Sixth Doctor, taking over the reins of the TARDIS in 1984?

A) Colin Firth

B) Colin Baker

C) Richard E Grant

7. The Seventh Doctor, played by Sylvester McCoy, travelled with companion Ace after meeting her on Iceworld where she was stranded, as a result of getting swept up in a time storm. What nickname did she affectionately call the Doctor during their adventures?

A) Mate

B) Doc

C) Professor

8. Paul McGann made his debut as the Eighth Doctor in 1996, almost seven years after the TV series of *Doctor Who* was cancelled. In which media form did his Doctor first appear?

A) A TV movie

B) An audio drama

C) A miniseries

Cast from the Past

Two Doctor actors had appeared in the
show before being cast as our time-
travelling hero. Both Colin Baker and Peter
Capaldi had appeared in *Who* previously
— Colin Baker alongside the Fifth Doctor
in 'Arc of Infinity' (1983) and Peter Capaldi
in a Tenth Doctor adventure, 'The Fires
of Pompeii' (2008). The Doctor later
discovered that they could subconsciously
choose their face when regenerating,
providing an in-universe explanation as
to why the Doctor might be played by an
actor who had been in the show before.

9. When *Doctor Who* returned to our TV screens in 2005, a new Doctor came with it. Christopher Eccleston played the leather jacket-clad hero – but for how many series did he stay in the role of the Doctor?

A) Three

B) One

C) Two

10. David Tennant took on the role of the titular Time Lord to play the character's tenth face. Which companion was present during his regeneration and stayed travelling with this Doctor until her goodbye in 'Doomsday'?

A) Sarah Jane Smith

B) Martha Jones

C) Rose Tyler

11. The Eleventh Doctor, played by Matt Smith, crashed onto our screens in 'The Eleventh Hour' (2010). Which food was his favourite after trying a host of dishes for the first time in his new body?

A) Fish fingers and custard

B) Beans on toast

C) Jelly Babies

12. An extra incarnation of the Doctor named the 'War Doctor' was revealed during *Doctor Who*'s fiftieth anniversary in 2013. Which famous British actor played this version of the Doctor?

A) Idris Elba

B) John Hurt

C) Alan Rickman

13. Peter Capaldi played the Twelfth Doctor from 2014–17. Which accent did this Doctor have?

A) Scottish

B) Irish

C) Cockney

14. In 2017, history was made when a woman was cast to play the Doctor for the first time. Which British actor took on the role and became the Thirteenth Doctor?

A) Jodie Foster

B) Jodie Whittaker

C) Jodie Comer

15. Jo Martin plays an incarnation of the Doctor from somewhere in the Time Lord's past. She first appeared during Series 12 in 2020. What name was given to her Doctor?

A) The Fugitive Doctor

B) The Prisoner Doctor

C) The Lost Doctor

16. Which *Sex Education* actor was announced in May 2022 to be taking on the role as a new incarnation of the Doctor?

A) Aimee Lou Wood

B) Ncuti Gatwa

C) Asa Butterfield

Costume Conundrum

Each Doctor has an iconic outfit to save the universe in. From scarves and long coats to bow ties and tweed jackets, the TARDIS' wardrobe is full of wacky clothes to match the Doctor's personality.

So, how well do you know Time Lord attire? Match the outfit accessories below to the correct Doctor.

Accessory	Answer

Accessory	Answer

Time for a Lady

When *Doctor Who* began to struggle
in the eighties and was at risk of
cancellation, the show's original creator,
Sydney Newman, suggested to the BBC
that they make some big changes –
including casting a female Doctor. The
change didn't materialise until over
thirty years later, in 2017.

Chapter Two

FRIENDS OF THE DOCTOR

The Doctor has had many travelling companions, all whisked away into a mysterious blue box and shown the wonders of the universe. Brave friends that become heroes by helping to save civilisations. People from across the galaxies enter the world of the Doctor and are never the same again. *Doctor Who* is largely about chosen family and these beloved friends become that, not only for the Doctor, but for us too.

In so many ways, the Doctor's companions symbolise the audience. When a new friend steps aboard the TARDIS, we arrive with them and get to see everything through fresh eyes. We relate to them, care for them, and root for them. We can see ourselves in their excitement as they set off across the stars, in their fear when faced with an evil adversary, and in their hope that the day will always be saved.

Companions to the Doctor show us that normal people can also be heroes. Just look at Donna Noble, a temp worker who felt she wasn't special. Or Yasmin Khan, a police officer in training who just wanted to make a difference. Generations of us have grown up seeing that we can be whatever and whoever we want to be because of these brilliant characters. They also teach us lessons – in bravery, courage and determination. They show us that whoever you are, you can make an impact on your world, no matter how small you start.

Where would the Doctor be without them? We all

need a friend to tell us when we've messed up, to help us through a tough time, or to even help save our lives (or at the very least, steer us down the right path). When the Doctor gets too selfish or caught up in the moment, they need a friend on hand to stop them and show them a better way. Nobody can know everything or be perfect, which is why our friends are the best of us, helping us to navigate our lives with love.

Our love for travelling with the Doctor has stayed ignited over the past six decades because we have access to countless worlds through the Doctor's friends. Each of them brings something new to the TARDIS and to us. A new experience to have, a new feeling to work through or new people to meet. No matter who your companion is, there's something to love and relate to in all of them.

So, which of the Doctor's friends do you know best? Find your favourites and test your knowledge in the following pages.

1. When we first enter the world of *Doctor Who* in 'An Unearthly Child', the Doctor is living in his TARDIS in a junkyard with his grandaughter. What is her name?

   A) Barbara

   B) Susan

   C) Vicki

2. Sarah Jane Smith first met the Doctor in 'The Time Warrior'. What was her occupation that led to her meeting the Third Doctor?

   A) Journalist

   B) Nurse

   C) Scientist

3. The Eleventh Doctor crashed the TARDIS into Amy Pond's back garden while recovering from his recent regeneration. Which village was her home located in, that was also the site of a crack in time?

   A) Shepperton

   B) Leadworth

   C) Medderton

4. Companion to the Seventh Doctor, Ace created her own explosive that she used to destroy a Dalek and later blow up a Cyber shuttle. What was the name that she gave it?

A) Ace Juice

B) Ex-plosive

C) Nitro-9

5. Martha Jones was training to be a doctor when she met the Tenth Doctor. Which space police aliens did they meet when the Royal Hope Hospital got transported to the moon?

A) The Slitheen

B) The Judoon

C) The Moxx of Balhoon

6. True or False? Rose Tyler joined the TARDIS in 2005, and travelled with two Doctors – the Ninth and Tenth incarnations.

7. The Doctor travels with friends from all over the Earth. What was the name of the Doctor's American friend, with whom he travelled during his fifth and sixth incarnations?

A) Peri Brown

B) Dorothy McShane

C) Verity Newman

8. Clara Oswald joined the Doctor on his travels in 2013 when she was a nanny. She later became a school teacher – which school did she work at that also featured in *Doctor Who*, way back in 1963?

A) Thames Hill

B) Grange Hill

C) Coal Hill

9. True or False? Spirited Seventh Doctor companion, Melanie Bush, was played by famous UK actor Bonnie Langford.

Cast from the Past: Companions

Karen Gillan (Amy Pond) and Freema Agyeman (Martha Jones) both appeared in *Doctor Who* before being cast as full-time companions. Freema appeared as Adeola Oshodi in the 2006 finale episodes, 'Army of Ghosts/Doomsday'. Her character was later linked to Martha, who told the Doctor that her cousin Adeola had died at the Battle of Canary Wharf. Gillan appeared in 2008's 'The Fires of Pompeii' alongside David Tennant, before being cast as Amy Pond in 2009.

10. River Song was the Doctor's wife, destined to meet him out of order as their timelines moved backwards. In which episode did the Doctor and River Song marry?

A) 'The Husbands of River Song'

B) 'The Honeymoon of River Song'

C) 'The Wedding of River Song'

11. Companion to the Third Doctor, Jo Grant was a UNIT employee who became the Doctor's assistant while he was working for the same organisation. In which story did she leave the Doctor, after they got to the bottom of a giant maggot mystery?

A) 'The Green Monsters'

B) 'The Green Hills'

C) 'The Green Death'

12. Romana was a fellow Time Lord who travelled with the Doctor after assisting him in his search to find and assemble the Key to Time. How many Romana regenerations did we meet on-screen?

   A) One

   B) Two

   C) Three

13. The Twelfth Doctor took Bill on as his companion after meeting her at St Luke's University, where he began giving her personal tutoring lessons. What was Bill's surname?

   A) Tyler

   B) Potts

   C) Pans

14. Yasmin Khan, Ryan Sinclair and Graham O'Brien joined the Thirteenth Doctor aboard the TARDIS in 2018 after defeating Tzim-Sha in Sheffield. What did the Doctor lovingly call her friends?

A) Her 'fam'

B) Her 'pals'

C) Her 'band'

15. Wilfred Mott, played by Bernard Cribbins, became a short-term companion to the Tenth Doctor during his final story, 'The End of Time'. Wilf was the grandfather of which friend of the Doctor?

A) Clara Oswald

B) Amy Pond

C) Donna Noble

Cast from the Past: Returning Actors

Occasionally, companion actors return to *Doctor Who* – as completely new characters. Jacqueline Hill, who played one of the Doctor's first friends, Barbara Wright, returned to the show fifteen years later to play Lexa in Fourth Doctor story 'Meglos'. Billie Piper also returned to the series four years after her final appearance as Rose Tyler to play The Moment in 2013's 'The Day of the Doctor'.

Which Companion Are You?

Most of us have imagined what we'd do if we were offered the trip of a lifetime around the universe. How would you react to your first planet or alien? You might have even practised your running, just in case the TARDIS came calling.

Every friend of the Doctor is different, taking on the wonders of being a time and space traveller in their own way. Take the quiz below to see which companion you are most like – after all, you never know when adventure might come knocking!

1. A mysterious time traveller enters your life and asks you to board their TARDIS and adventure with them. What is your response?

   A) You weren't asked – you stowed away on the TARDIS while investigating strange happenings and stayed for further travels.

   B) You were looking for a way out – you say yes without a second thought!

C) You say no at first, because your family
need you, but you change your mind
when you realise it also travels in time.

D) You've seen enough of the Doctor to know
that you'll say yes to the invitation and
never leave.

**2. You have the entirety of time and space at
your feet. Where would you choose to go for
your first adventure in the TARDIS?**

A) The Middle Ages

B) London, 1963

C) The distant future, to see the end of
the Earth

D) An alien planet

3. How would others describe you?

A) Confident, clever and brave. You're never
one to put up with anybody else's rubbish
and you're a brilliant leader. Sometimes
you come across as a bit cold – but only

because you're so fiercely protective and loving.

B) Under that tough exterior you're kind, loyal and deeply courageous. You like to take charge and sometimes act without thinking, but you're a fast learner and will always remain loyal to those you care about.

C) Kind, caring and inquisitive, you're protective of those around you and can make friends in any situation. You're deeply empathetic, sometimes to your own disadvantage, but can also take a stand when needed.

D) You're wildly ambitious and want to rise to the top. Although you have many insecurities, you're a brilliant friend and are talented at solving any problem. Always asking questions, you're curious and have a brave exterior – you just need to remember your own brilliance.

FRIENDS OF THE DOCTOR

4. You're stuck in an alien base with no signal, no Doctor and no way out. Do you:

A) Investigate your surroundings and try to find a logical solution.

B) Blow the base up with your homemade explosive.

C) Use your under-seven gymnastics bronze medal skills and try to kick the door down.

D) Wonder what the Doctor would do, and then do exactly that.

6. The Doctor leaves you on a distant planet by accident and you have no idea if they'll be back. Do you:

A) Make a life for yourself and become a defender of your new home.

B) Get a job in hospitality and try to figure out a way off the planet.

C) Create a teleport to jump across the universe to wherever the Doctor is.

D) Accumulate local knowledge and make your own way back to the Doctor.

5. The Doctor's companions have distinct wardrobes to match their personalities. Which best describes your wardrobe?

A) Whatever is on trend and practical.

B) Oversized shirts and baseball jackets.

C) Comfy, casual jeans and hoodies.

D) Leather jackets and chunky boots.

8. You're faced with a Dalek for the first time, and it tells you it needs your help. You know the Dalek is a deadly enemy of the Doctor's – how do you handle the situation?

A) Talk your way out of the situation – violence is never the answer.

B) Whack it with a baseball bat.

C) Comfort it and try to reason with it – after all, everything has feelings, right?

D) Use your detective skills to figure out what it wants and de-escalate the situation.

9. You have to cease travelling with the Doctor. What has made you leave the TARDIS and your best friend?

A) You've been left on Earth because the Doctor has business to attend to, but you didn't want to leave.

B) The reason is unclear – but you tell everyone a different story.

C) You get stuck in a parallel universe with no way for the Doctor to rescue you.

D) You'll never leave the Doctor – you love them too much.

7. Which fearsome foe would you most like to help the Doctor to defeat?

A) The Daleks

B) The Cybermen

C) The Slitheen

D) The Master

(Mostly As) Sarah Jane Smith

Smart, brave and confident, you're most like Sarah Jane Smith. You're not afraid to speak your mind or uncover the truth and you're top of your game in your field. You lead and others follow, making you a great mentor and friend.

(Mostly Bs) Ace

You're most like Ace – streetwise, explosive and a fiercely loyal pal. Your determination and courage are your strengths and your bold exterior shines through wherever you go.

(Mostly Cs) Rose Tyler

Most like Rose Tyler, you're kind and helpful like a warm hug, and not afraid to do the right thing when everybody else runs away. Your heart is big and your smile touches everybody you meet.

(Mostly Ds) Yasmin Khan

Clever, determined and courageous, you're most like Yasmin Khan. People find you grounding and naturally gravitate towards you. Your willingness to keep trying means your ambition is achievable – you just have to believe in yourself!

The Lonely Traveller

The Doctor hadn't adventured without a travelling pal until 1976's 'The Deadly Assassin', when the Time Lord returned home to Gallifrey. This was the only classic series story to feature the Doctor without a companion. However, new series episodes have occasionally seen the Doctor travel alone, meeting new friends without taking them along for a TARDIS trip.

Chapter Three

THE TARDIS

Where would you go if you had a time ship that could take you anywhere? What would you see? Would you travel back into history to meet Vincent van Gogh, or would you speed into the future to see what became of the Earth? Maybe you'd travel to another galaxy and visit an alien planet, or discover a new world? It may not be possible in our lifetime, but we get to have those experiences through our TV screens because of the TARDIS.

Whether you're simply a fan of the beautiful console rooms or know the mechanics of the TARDIS inside out, the Doctor's trusty ship has an endless history and a perpetual bank of stories to dive into.

The TARDIS is a signal of hope across the universe. A box that can take you anywhere at any time in history. A magical shelter in which everything is possible for anyone.

Everybody knows the police telephone box, standing tall on street corners, will have danger and adventure not far away... The ship is something of a safe space, for the characters in our beloved show and for us when we want to escape. A place of protection and a home, it opens up our world and makes it bigger, helping us to experience more than what our lives might grant us – and even inspires us to get out and explore. What better way to discover a taste for travel and new experiences than a ride in the TARDIS?

Without the TARDIS, the Doctor wouldn't be the

saviour of space and time. Over the years, the ship has always taken our hero where they need to go, even if it's not what they had planned. To planets that need saving, enemies that need defeating and friends that need meeting, it is the machine that drives the beating heart of *Doctor Who*.

The TARDIS itself is a work of art. The best part about it is that we will never know every single treasure or room inside! A wooden beauty, filled to the brim with endless possibilities, it is also a living being that can communicate with its passengers and control itself. This particular spaceship has become another beloved character, another aspect of *Who* lore that makes *Doctor Who* so special.

So, do you know your TARDIS facts? Try the following questions – and take notes – just in case a blue box ever shows up on your doorstep...

1. The Doctor's home and travel machine is called the TARDIS – which is actually an acronym for the ship's real name. What does TARDIS stand for?

A) Time and Rhyme Dimension in Space

B) Time and Relative Dimension in Space

C) Totally and Radically Driving in Space

2. The TARDIS has a function that is *supposed* to make the ship change, so that it blends into its surroundings whenever it lands in a new place. What is the broken function called?

A) The Chameleon Circuit

B) The Blending Circuit

C) The Changing Circuit

3. Time Lord technology means that the TARDIS is...

A) Bigger on the outside

B) Bigger on the inside

C) Bigger than the sun

TARDIS Food

The First Doctor's TARDIS featured a food machine. The machine could create flavoured bars of artificial sustenance that tasted like whatever meal you fancied. The Doctor used it to make bacon and eggs for companions Barbara and Ian during 'The Daleks', and milk and water were also stored inside so that TARDIS travellers could stay hydrated!

4. The TARDIS is powered by an energy source from the Eye of Harmony. What is the name of the energy source?

A) Eon energy

B) Artron energy

C) Harmony energy

5. True or False? The Thirteenth Doctor's TARDIS had a biscuit dispenser, most commonly providing the TARDIS crew with custard creams.

6. The Doctor has a close relationship with their ship, often talking to and stroking it lovingly. What does the Doctor sometimes call the TARDIS?

A) Lovely

B) Cutie

C) Sexy

7. The TARDIS has been home to many of the Doctor's friends, who often even have their own bedroom on the ship. Which companion did the TARDIS famously not get along with, due to the impossible nature of her being scattered throughout the Doctor's timeline?

A) Clara Oswald

B) Dodo Chaplet

C) Susan Foreman

8. The Doctor ran away from their home planet to see the stars. How did the Doctor originally acquire their TARDIS to begin these travels?

A) They were gifted it by the Time Lords

B) They stole it from Gallifrey

C) They built it on Gallifrey

Snap to Open

The TARDIS can be opened by a snap of the Doctor's fingers. However, they did not find out about this ability until River Song revealed the secret in 2008's 'Forest of the Dead'. Since then, the Doc has snapped their fingers to open the TARDIS doors several times rather than using a key – very handy in emergencies!

9. Every vehicle needs power, including the TARDIS. Where does the Doctor occasionally take the TARDIS to refuel?

A) The space petrol station

B) UNIT HQ in London

C) A rift in space and time in Cardiff Bay

10. There are many different TARDISes knocking about the universe. There are even other people who have their own – like the Doctor's friend, Clara Oswald, or their frenemy, the Master. Which kind of TARDIS is the Doctor's?

A) Type 40

B) Mark one

C) TARDIS 500

11. True or False? The TARDIS telepathically translates spoken and written language using a translation circuit, meaning the Doctor and their friends will always understand anyone new that they meet – human or alien!

12. The TARDIS Console room often changes in design while retaining its basic features. Which Doctor's was made of coral-like structures?

A) The First Doctor

B) The Ninth and Tenth

C) The Fifth Doctor

13. During 'The Doctor's Wife' (2011), a woman named Idris becomes host to the soul of the TARDIS, enabling the ship to interact with and speak to the Doctor through her. Who played Idris?

A) Olivia Colman

B) Katherine Kelly

C) Suranne Jones

14. The TARDIS interior often has round panels on the walls, giving the ship a futuristic vibe. What does the Doctor often call these?

A) The round things

B) The hole things

C) The wall things

15. The TARDIS is disguised as a 1960s police box. Which instructional phrase is written on a sign on the front door?

A) 'Pull to close'

B) 'Pull to open'

C) 'Push open'

16. Many of the Doctor's friends have attempted to learn how the TARDIS works over the years. Which of them knew how to fly the TARDIS – sometimes better than the Doctor did?

A) River Song

B) Bill Potts

C) Ryan Sinclair

17. True or False? The TARDIS has many passengers and friends that call it home – but the Doctor is the only one allowed a key to the endless space-time ship.

Origins of the TARDIS Interior

The first-ever TARDIS console room was designed by Peter Brachacki, who was a BBC production designer in the sixties. His concept included a moving time column, roundels on the walls and objects from throughout history scattered about to create the impression that the ship was a time-travelling machine. The console room has been redesigned many times over the years, but these key features are always present in some way.

18. The TARDIS console is full of buttons, levers and scanners – and the Eleventh Doctor's version even featured a ketchup and mustard dispenser! What is the name of the column in the middle of the TARDIS console that usually moves up and down when the ship is in flight?

A) The Rotation Column

B) The Time Rotor

C) The Dematerialisation Column

TARDIS Wordsearch

The TARDIS has many names and descriptions attached to its legend. The technology behind the ship is vast, complicated and fascinating. From the many rooms to explore to the details in the console, it is a world of many wonders.

Search this TARDIS-filled grid to find all of the words relating to our favourite time machine.

Roundel

Artron energy

Console

Police Box

Ghost Monument

Zero room

Eye of Harmony

Type Forty

The Rift

Idris

P	A	R	T	R	O	N	E	N	E	R	G	Y	T
N	T	M	O	O	R	O	R	E	Z	R	E	N	T
C	Y	T	L	E	S	R	S	S	Y	O	Y	O	M
O	P	E	Y	O	P	N	I	R	L	M	E	D	I
N	E	N	A	O	T	T	R	E	L	O	O	L	R
S	F	H	O	N	F	E	D	E	N	P	F	T	Y
O	O	E	T	D	I	N	I	R	F	I	H	O	O
L	R	O	N	P	U	I	M	S	S	N	A	O	F
E	T	I	I	O	E	O	T	D	F	S	R	C	T
O	Y	B	R	C	L	N	B	H	O	O	M	S	M
O	T	N	E	M	U	N	O	M	T	S	O	H	G
L	T	H	E	R	I	F	T	R	R	O	N	F	P
R	G	H	E	O	S	E	I	E	T	E	Y	E	Y
O	P	O	L	I	C	E	B	O	X	Y	Y	X	I

Chapter Four

ALIENS & ADVERSARIES

The world of *Doctor Who* is vast and endless, filled to the brim with aliens, monsters and villains. The Doctor has spent their many regenerations battling them, reasoning with them and, sometimes, even saving them. We've met creatures from the far future and the distant past. Some aren't even alien and inhabited the Earth before we did. Other adversaries are terrifying, haunting us for weeks after an episode. Occasionally, we might even be fooled by adorable appearances too.

Doctor Who has had a lot to teach us through the bad guys that the Doctor has met. We've watched the impact of division and hatred, and have been shown the importance of sticking together. Other times, we've been taught that responding with kindness and empathy instead of violence is a better way. We've witnessed wars and invasions and watched the Doctor and their friends save the day every time, filling us with hope about our world and the universe beyond it.

Aliens and adversaries don't just exist for lessons though, but also for the fun and the excitement. We love watching strange monsters bumble around in their rubber costumes, or laughing at comedians caked in layers of prosthetics to become alien creatures to us. Nothing beats the thrill of experiencing the weird and wonderful ways in which these characters communicate and live.

We must enjoy being scared too, though. Do you remember hiding behind a cushion in the dark while a

Weeping Angel or a terrifying Yeti appeared on your screen? Maybe that fear calms our anxiety about the real world. After all, at least we haven't got terrifying beasts or robots or ghosts terrorising our homes and picking off the people we love. Maybe these monsters embody our scary emotions and *Doctor Who* is the vehicle that drives us to face them. They're also what makes the Doctor the saviour of the universe, and what makes the companions so relatable. They bring other-worldliness to our lives, which means we can escape into a different story, feel new things and maybe even face our fears.

The questions in this chapter cover an array of alien species, monsters and villains from across the Whoniverse – aside from the Daleks and Cybermen, who we'll get into later. Can you figure out the answers to these creature conundrums and spot your favourite within these pages?

1. When *Doctor Who* returned to our screens in 2005, the show introduced us to countless new creatures and monsters from all over the universe. Which farting alien family did the Doctor and Rose discover had invaded London during 'Aliens of London/World War Three', who disguised themselves as humans by wearing their skin?

   A) The Mire

   B) The Jagrafess

   C) The Slitheen

2. Shape-changing creatures, the Zygons, first appeared in 'Terror of the Zygons' in 1975. They later returned to the show in 'The Day of the Doctor' (2013) to once again attempt to colonise the Earth. Which incarnation of the Doctor first encountered the Zygons?

   A) The Fourth Doctor

   B) The Third Doctor

   C) The Tenth Doctor

3. The Weeping Angels first appeared in 'Blink' (2007), where Sally Sparrow battled the stone statue creatures with only a video of the Doctor to help her. What action must you NOT do when in the presence of a Weeping Angel, or they may zap you back in time?

A) Smile

B) Blink

C) Sneeze

4. True or False? The Third Doctor, the Fifth Doctor and the Thirteenth Doctor have all met the Sea Devils during their TV adventures.

5. The Doctor has met hundreds of creatures – huge, small, good and bad. Which tiny but hungry alien did the Thirteenth Doctor encounter aboard the *Tsuranga* ship during 'The Tsuranga Conundrum' (2018)?

A) Beep the Meep

B) The Pting

C) The Adipose

No Bug-eyed Monsters!

When *Doctor Who* was created by Sydney Newman in 1963, he wanted to avoid putting 'bug-eyed monsters' in the show at all costs. Newman believed the outer-space elements of *Doctor Who* should be as accurate to what was factually known at the time as possible. He didn't even want the Daleks to appear, but producer Verity Lambert convinced him otherwise – and they went on to prove themselves by capturing the imagination and hearts of the nation!

6. The Sontarans are a clone race obsessed with war, who first appeared in 'The Time Warrior' (1973). What is their chilling war cry, used before they enter into battle?

A) Sontar-ha!

B) Sontaroo!

C) Sontar Strong!

7. The Doctor and Rose met the Abzorbaloff in 'Love & Monsters' (2006), after members of LINDA had been cruelly absorbed by the giant green creature. Which famous UK comedian portrayed the Abzorbaloff?

A) Nick Frost

B) Simon Pegg

C) Peter Kay

8. The Doctor and their friends have thwarted countless alien plots to harm our planet. Which alien race possessed plastic shop-window dummies to invade Earth, twice in the seventies and again in the early noughties?

A) The Rutans

B) The Nestene Consciousness

C) The Ood

9. The Eleventh Doctor encountered the Silence on multiple occasions throughout his regeneration, first meeting the terrifying creatures during 'The Impossible Astronaut' (2011). How did the Doctor and his friends keep track of how many Silents they had seen after forgetting them?

A) They wrote tally marks on their body

B) They kept an Excel spreadsheet

C) They wrote it down in a notebook

10. The Doctor first encountered the deadly Ice Warriors during their second incarnation, after landing aboard the Britannicus Base with Jamie and Victoria. Which planet did the Ice Warriors originate from?

A) Earth

B) Mars

C) Jupiter

11. The Ood made their *Doctor Who* debut in 'The Impossible Planet' (2006), where they met the Tenth Doctor and Rose while serving humans aboard Sanctuary Base 6. Who possessed the Ood to brutally murder members of the Sanctuary Base crew, one by one?

A) The Doctor

B) Brian the Ood

C) The Beast

12. True or False? The Silurians, who have encountered many incarnations of the Doctor over the years, originally come from the planet Siluria.

13. The Fourth Doctor, Romana and K9 encountered the Nimon in 'The Horns of Nimon' (1979), when the TARDIS crashed into a spaceship with a suspicious cargo. The Nimons resemble which mythical creature?

A) Cyclops

B) Minotaur

C) Dragon

14. The Doctor and Donna Noble first met when Donna was transported into the TARDIS. The pair then discovered that the Racnoss was at the heart of the mystery. Which episode did the Racnoss Earth invasion happen in?

A) 'The Runaway Bride'

B) 'The Fires of Pompeii'

C) 'Partners In Crime'

Mythical Monsters

Doctor Who has often drawn inspiration from mythical or fairy-tale baddies to inform its aliens or monsters. The Fourth and Eleventh Doctors met vampires in 'State of Decay' and 'The Vampires of Venice', The Tenth Doctor met a werewolf in 2006's 'Tooth and Claw', and the Twelfth Doctor met a mummy in the form of the Foretold in 2014's 'Mummy on the Orient Express'.

15. Which *Doctor Who* villain first appeared in 1967's 'The Abominable Snowmen' and later returned in 2012/13 to try and take the Doctor down during their Eleventh incarnation?

    A) The Great Being

    B) The Great Intelligence

    C) The Great Mastermind

Monster Madness

Think you know your Sensorites from your Sea Devils? Your Vervoids from your Vespiform? If you think you could identify any species in the universe, take the test below and guess which *Doctor Who* creature or villain is being described based on the clues.

1. These creatures have an odd name, but a peaceful nature. Their main facial feature is pink, tentacle-like fronds. They are bonded together through a telepathic hive mind and naturally carry their second brain – the hindbrain – in their hands. Often they are found enslaved by other races, most notably by humans. The Tenth Doctor was the first incarnation to meet them.

2. This race originally inhabited the Earth, long before humanity did. They have a reptilian appearance, sometimes with green or brown scaly skin that comes in many variations. The Third Doctor was the first to meet them.

The Eleventh and Twelfth Doctors were close friends with a particular member of this race, who often helped save the world.

3. These potato-headed aliens are a clone race obsessed with war, often found in battle or preparing for one. They love to destroy civilisations and take over planets. They have three fingers on each hand and brown or grey skin. The Third Doctor and Sarah Jane were the first to encounter them. The Tenth and Thirteenth Doctors have also fought them.

4. You won't remember these towering monsters if you look away from them. They have eyes deep-set far into their heads and a distinct lack of mouth in their skull-like faces. The versions that the Eleventh Doctor encountered were dressed in black suits. These creatures are actually priests — *and, sorry, what was I talking about?*

5. Tiny and made from fat, these little aliens are adorable to look at and resemble fluffy marshmallows or blobs. These creatures reproduce on 'nursery' worlds, where fat and tissue from natives of the planet are converted into babies. These babies jump from the body at night and make their way back to their parents ... Cute, right?

6. This race resembles a giant, fluffy humanoid dog. They are species bonded with the human race – meaning they have to protect us at all costs! They helped to do so when the Earth was in danger from the Flux, while the Thirteenth Doctor tried to figure out how to save the universe.

Dan Lewis was species bonded with Karvanista, a member of this race who had previously been a companion to the Fugitive Doctor.

7. These brutal aliens are known as the galactic space police, enforcing the law savagely throughout space. They have rhino-like heads and are usually found wearing leather space suits and helmets. Their language entirely consists of one-syllable words. Multiple Doctors have encountered these creatures on their adventures.

8. Resembling giant ants, these creatures can be found on the planet Vortis. Unintelligent and easily controlled, they stand on two legs and communicate by screeching and rubbing their legs together. The First Doctor, Vicki, Ian and Barbara met them when the TARDIS was dragged down to Vortis in the 1965 adventure, 'The Web Planet'.

Creature Actors

Some *Doctor Who* actors returned to
the show as a monster or creature
after previously playing a human role.
Anjli Mohindra, who played Rani in
The Sarah Jane Adventures, returned to
the Whoniverse in 2020 to play the Queen
of the Skithra in 'Nikola Tesla's Night of
Terror'. Conversely, Adjoa Andoh made
her *Who* debut in prosthetics as Sister Jatt
in 2006, before returning to the show
as Martha's mum, Francine in Series 3
of New *Who*.

Chapter Five

DEADLY DALEKS

The Daleks are the Doctor's most famous enemy. As old as *Doctor Who* itself, the pepper pot maniacs have been threatening the galaxies for almost sixty years, with no sign of stopping. Everybody knows what a Dalek is, with their signature plunger arm and menacing eye stalk. We all know their catchphrase and their chilling voices. They're an enemy to every incarnation of the Doctor, always surviving and always returning – much to our excitement!

Most of us have a memory of the Daleks etched into our minds. It might be the first time that you saw them on-screen: a Dalek floating up out of the Thames in 'The Dalek Invasion of Earth', or the Cult of Skaro menacingly exiting *The Sphere* in 'Army of Ghosts'. Or maybe you've met one face to face at live events such as *Doctor Who Experience* or *Doctor Who: Time Fracture*. You might also have a favourite colour or design, a sixties blue and silver or a 2010 Paradigm Dalek, maybe? Whatever variation, their terrifying silhouette remains the same, and has cemented them as a figure of fear and universal domination.

It seems fitting for the Doctor to have an enemy so perpetual. In order to continually portray that evil cannot prevail, our hero has to repeatedly battle them in new ways. The Doctor always wins, but evil always returns. Maybe that is how we should look to experience life – keep on trying and facing down hatred because, eventually, we will win. Evil will always come back to try and bring us down, but we should never give up. This is what the Daleks continually symbolise to us. Their continued presence shows that division does not serve us and the Doctor's determination to stop them tells us to keep fighting for what is right in our lives and our world.

It's a thrill to watch every time the Daleks come up with a new plan, only to be thwarted by the Doctor. Those cheer-worthy moments as they're pulled into a void or when their technology is used against them keep us returning to the show time and time again.

Our favourite villains have a rich and complicated history and that makes them a fascinating enemy – but you don't have to know this history to enjoy their iconic appearances. All you need is a sofa to hide behind, a hero like the Doctor and the hope that these maniacal machines will never conquer the world!

Do you have what it takes to defeat a Dalek? Test your knowledge and prepare with these questions. You'll need to know everything about them, just in case you ever come eye to eyestalk in the future ...

1. The Daleks were created in 1963, alongside the launch of *Doctor Who*, appearing in the second serial of the show. Which *Who* writer came up with idea of the Daleks?

A) David Whitaker

B) Russell T Davies

C) Terry Nation

2. The Doctor first visited the Daleks' home planet in 1963's 'The Daleks'. Which planet do the Daleks come from?

A) Mondas

B) Saturn

C) Skaro

3. In 1975's 'Genesis of the Daleks', the Fourth Doctor and his companions Sarah Jane and Harry discover the origins of the deadly Daleks and meet their creator. Which scientist created the Daleks?

A) Davros

B) Caan

C) Einstein

The Ultimate Enemy

The Daleks have met more incarnations of the Doctor on-screen than any other villain. Every regeneration has fought the Daleks during their television adventures apart from the Eighth Doctor and the Fugitive Doctor. The Daleks did make an appearance in the Eighth Doctor's debut, the 1996 TV movie *Doctor Who*, however, this incarnation did not meet them during the adventure.

4. Every killing machine must have a war cry, catchphrase or trademark. What is the Dalek's catchphrase which they usually scream before killing their enemies?

A) Examinate!

B) Exterminate!

C) Delete!

5. The Daleks' outer casing is a machine in which a living creature is housed. What creature is found inside a Dalek?

A) A baby

B) A mutant

C) A squid

6. The Daleks were created as a way for a race at war to survive. Which race did the Daleks originate from?

A) Kaleds

B) Humans

C) Martians

7. Which Doctor met the Daleks when they invaded Manhattan during the construction of the Empire State Building in 1930?

A) The Thirteenth Doctor

B) The Fourth Doctor

C) The Tenth Doctor

8. True or False? Dalek casing is a means of travel and protection for the creature living inside. The casing is made of a material called Dalekanium.

9. Daleks come in many different colours, which sometimes determine their rank or mean they have a specific name or title. What colour casing does Dalek Sec have?

A) Gold

B) Black

C) Green

Dalek Movie Madness

The Daleks got their own set of movies during the 1960s, completely separate from the main TV show. The Doctor was played by Peter Cushing, and the films even included Bernard Cribbins (who also played Wilf, companion to the Tenth Doctor)! *Dr. Who and the Daleks* was released in 1965 – this period was aptly named 'Dalekmania' due to how huge the Daleks became in popular culture, thanks to *Doctor Who* and the Dalek films.

10. Many of the Doctor's friends have battled the Daleks alongside our hero. Which friend of the Doctor's turned out to have actually been converted into a Dalek in 'Asylum of the Daleks' (2012)?

A) Oswin Oswald

B) Brian Pond

C) River Song

11. The Daleks have invaded Earth countless times. In which story did the Daleks threaten London in 1963?

A) 'Day of the Daleks'

B) 'Dalek'

C) 'Remembrance of the Daleks'

12. Sometimes the Doctor faces whole legions of Daleks, but it doesn't take many to threaten the universe. How many Daleks appear in 'Resolution' (2019)?

A) Three

B) Two

C) One

13. The Daleks have landed in many periods throughout the Earth's history, ready to conquer and destroy. In which episode did the Daleks disguise themselves as servants, serving tea to Winston Churchill?

    A) 'Victory of the Daleks'

    B) 'War of the Daleks'

    C) 'Evolution of the Daleks'

14. Which companion to the Doctor touched a Dalek, which absorbed some of her DNA, ultimately resulting in its death because it was no longer 'pure'?

    A) Sarah Jane Smith

    B) Rose Tyler

    C) Amy Pond

15. True or False? Companion Jo Grant never met a Dalek while adventuring with the Doctor.

16. The Daleks measure time differently to us on Earth. What unit do they use?

A) Rels

B) Reels

C) Bills

17. Throughout their history, the Daleks have used spaceships to get around the universe and begin battles and wars. What shape does a Dalek spaceship usually take?

A) Sphere

B) Saucer

C) Cylinder

Scrambled Daleks

Words to Unscramble	Answer
OASRK	
RIAXTEETMEN	
LRPNGEU	
TYAKLEES	
ROSVAD	
AEDLK EERMPOR	
UTCL FO ASOKR	
IMTE ARW	
NKGCUSIT	
TRIEYLA BMBO	
ALKED ESC	
KAELD AACN	
KDALE TAUNMT	
ERLS	

Dalek Design

The Daleks were ingeniously designed by Ray Cusick, a BBC staff designer on *Doctor Who* in the sixties. Ray took on the role of creating the deadliest villains in the galaxy after director Ridley Scott – who was also a designer at the BBC at the time – had to drop the task due to a conflict in his schedule!

Chapter Six

HISTORICAL
ADVENTURES

Doctor Who was born with a purpose: to educate its audience. Back in 1963, the producers of the show wanted *Who* to inspire and teach viewers by taking us back into the past to learn about our history, or to the future to discover science. Over the years, the TARDIS has opened doors so that we can learn from our past and explore what has made us who we are today.

For some of us, *Doctor Who*'s historical adventures have uncovered little-known stories that we may never have discovered if not for the TARDIS. We've learnt about Noor Inayat Khan, Britain's first Muslim war hero, and have even met Nefertiti, Queen of Egypt. We've discovered the life of Madame de Pompadour and the story of the 'King of Pirates', Henry Avery. All real people from our history with their extraordinary lives, who we may never have heard about if the Doctor hadn't introduced us to them.

Other episodes focus on famous monarchs or memorable historical figures; writers such as William Shakespeare and Charles Dickens, events like World War II and periods such as Victorian England. There's nothing more satisfying than watching the Tenth Doctor and Rose banter with Queen Victoria, or the Eleventh Doctor and Amy help post-Impressionist painter Vincent van Gogh. Their stories might have been known to us, but *Doctor Who* gave us a way to see these figures in a brand-new light.

Sometimes our limitless show has filled in gaps from the past that have never been fully explained. What happened to novelist Agatha Christie during the 11 days she disappeared? What is the truth behind the Williamson Tunnels? *Doctor Who* has cleverly filled in parts of history that nobody knows the answer to, and the result adds to the wonderful notion that the Doctor has always been looking after us and our world.

There are certain periods or people that might particularly pique our interest now because *Doctor Who* brought us their stories. We might want to find out more about the French Revolution because we explored it through the eyes of the First Doctor and his friends. Maybe you've taken an interest in the Crimean War because the Thirteenth Doctor introduced us to the brilliant British-Jamaican nurse Mary Seacole. Perhaps you've littered your home with prints of van Gogh paintings, or Mary Shelley's books. That's the beauty of a show like *Doctor Who*: it makes our world bigger and more exciting.

So, how well do you know the TARDISes travels throughout history? Adventure through the following questions and revisit the past with the Doctor. From the eruption of Vesuvius to the height of World War II, strap yourself in for a history lesson …

1. The Doctor has had their fair share of romantic relationships and even a couple of marriages. Which queen did the Tenth Doctor reluctantly marry in 'The Day of the Doctor' (2013)?

- A) Queen Victoria
- B) Elizabeth I
- C) Elizabeth II

2. The Doctor loves to give every new TARDIS traveller a trip back in time to remember. Which civil rights activist did the Thirteenth Doctor, Yaz, Ryan and Graham meet on their first trip into the past?

3. The First Doctor and his friends often visited Earth's past. Which of his companions was mistaken for the ancient god Yetexa when the gang travelled to fifteenth-century Mexico, in 1964 story 'The Aztecs'?

- A) Barbara Wright
- B) Susan Foreman
- C) Dodo Chaplet

4. Which companion accidentally joined the Third Doctor in travelling to the thirteenth century, where the Sontarans made their first appearance?

5. The Doctor and Amy Pond met Vincent van Gogh in 'Vincent and the Doctor' (2010). Which painting did the struggling artist dedicate to Amy, which was later displayed in the Musée d'Orsay in Paris?

A) *The Starry Night*

B) *Wheatfield with Crows*

C) *Vase with Twelve Sunflowers*

6. Occasionally, the Doctor bumps into famous leaders and warriors from our history, too. Which Doctor met Richard the Lionheart?

A) The First Doctor

B) The Second Doctor

C) The Tenth Doctor

Curtis and the Doctor

Love Actually and *Notting Hill* writer
Richard Curtis penned the 2010 episode
'Vincent and the Doctor', intending it as
a tribute to his late sister Belinda, who
was a fan of Vincent van Gogh. The plot
tackled the story of van Gogh's life and its
powerful and realistic portrayal of mental
health has made it a fan favourite.

7. Which Twelfth Doctor episode answered the question of what happened to the Ninth Legion of the Roman army?

    A) 'Thin Ice'

    B) 'The Eaters of Light'

    C) 'Survival'

8. Where did the Tenth Doctor and Rose Tyler intend to land in the episode 'Tooth and Claw', before accidentally ending up in Victorian Scotland?

    A) Sheffield, 2009

    B) Sheffield, 1969

    C) Sheffield, 1979

9. When the Thirteenth Doctor and her fam landed by Lake Geneva, they met English novelist Mary Shelley and her friends at Villa Diodati. Which creature did they encounter there, that Shelley described as a 'Modern Prometheus'?

10. Some of the Doctor's companions had their own favourite eras, or people, from history. Which Roman Emperor did Clara Oswald have a poster of when she was a teenager?

A) Marcus Aurelius

B) Claudius Caesar

C) Nero

11. The Tenth Doctor and Donna Noble solved a mystery with detective writer Agatha Christie after landing in Surrey in 1926 – where they encountered the Vespiform. Which Earth insect did the Vespiform resemble?

A) Beetle

B) Wasp

C) Ant

12. Who wrote 'The Empty Child/The Doctor Dances', in which the Ninth Doctor and Rose Tyler land in London during the Blitz?

13. The Thirteenth Doctor has met some brilliant women who changed the world. Which iconic mathematician helped the Doctor fend off the Master in 'Spyfall' (2020)?

14. In which story did H G Wells have an adventure with the Doctor that inspired him to go on and write science fiction novels?

A) 'Time Flight'

B) 'Time Fracture'

C) 'Timelash'

15. True or False? The Tenth Doctor and Martha Jones were zapped back and stuck in 1969, leaving Sally Sparrow to deal with the deadly Weeping Angels during 'Blink' (2007).

16. The Twelfth Doctor and Bill Potts visited a frost fair in 1814, finding a mysterious creature causing terror under the ice. Which river was the frost fair held upon?

17. The Doctor has met countless friends and enemies while traversing the Earth's history. In what village during the nineteenth century did the Sixth Doctor first meet the Rani?

A) Killingsworth

B) Murdersworth

C) Leadworth

18. The TARDIS loves to drop the Doctor off outside the doors of famous writers. Which witchy aliens tried to cast their spell over Shakespeare in an attempt to free their race and take the Earth?

A Villa Full of History

'The Haunting of Villa Diodati' (2020) holds the highest number of historical figures within a New *Who* episode, featuring a whopping eight people from our past – including Mary Shelley, Percy Shelley, Lord Byron and their friends as they took their famous 1816 trip to Lake Geneva.

History Mystery

Whether you've travelled with the Tenth Doctor to ancient Pompeii or with the Third Doctor to the Middle Ages, there's been an historical adventure for everyone. There's a whole host of icons from our past that we've met through the Doctor, each teaching us the lessons of what came before and bringing us closer to our history.

So how well do you know your historical figures in *Doctor Who*? Test your TARDIS travelling knowledge by matching the person from history to the episode they appeared in.

Mary Seacole

'Rosa'

'War of the Sontarans'

Napoleon Bonaparte

'Nikola Tesla's Night of Terror'

Agatha Christie

'The Unquiet Dead'

'The Haunting of Villa Diodati'

Martin Luther King

Richard Nixon

'The Unicorn and the Wasp'

'The Reign of Terror'

Queen Nefertiti

Mary Shelley

'The Impossible Astronaut/ Day of the Moon'

Charles Dickens

Nikola Tesla

'Dinosaurs on a Spaceship'

'The Girl in the Fireplace'

Madame de Pompadour

Historical Firsts

The 1964 story 'Marco Polo' was the first
instance in *Doctor Who* where a famous
person from our history was featured.
The serial introduced us to explorer
Marco Polo and Emperor Kublai Khan –
and saw the Doctor and his friends halt
an attempted assassination against the
Mongolian Emperor in 1289.

Chapter Seven

THE MASTER

The Master is the ultimate villain, rarely redeeming themselves and always returning for revenge. So are they the Doctor's friend or their enemy? Usually causing chaos and trying to take our hero down, they most certainly fall into the latter category. And yet, we're often rooting for the pair to finally make amends: for the Doctor and the Master to come together on the same side.

The rival Time Lord has been gracing our screens since the Third Doctor's era and has had us on the edge of our seats for over fifty years. They've created dastardly plots to destroy the Doctor, attempted to end the universe itself, and even murdered the entirety of Gallifrey. They've brought the Doctor together with their friends, but have also hurt them in the most terrible ways. What is worse than a friend who turns against you? What hurts more than when somebody you care about decides that they hate you?

The Master reflects possibly the darkest parts of all of us. Our desire to be better than others, our jealousy and our anger. How we sometimes have a need to destroy what is around us when we don't know how to handle our emotions. They symbolise those stubborn tendencies to leave the broken parts of ourselves unfixed, because we are too scared to admit to them. Maybe we secretly feel for the Master because we've all been the underdog? Perhaps we despise them because we've learnt to be better and know that it is possible? We're conflicted by this character because, sometimes, we wish we could just act on our darkest feelings, but we know that we never would.

They also bring out the best in us; because we know what is right, and the Doctor taking down evil helps us to see that we can do the same. The relationship between these beloved characters shows us what might happen if we let ourselves get lost or stuck in our hurt. It also shows the viewer that we must keep trying to forgive and make good, even when we've been wounded over and over. What better way to prove to ourselves that we *can* be better?

There's also such fun to be had with a character so psychotic! The unpredictability, the camp outfits, the flirting and the savagery. Sometimes there's nothing better than a classic villain. We never tire of watching the Doctor and the Master face off against each other.

Whichever incarnation of the Master you love the most, there's a celebration of your favourite villain to be had within the following questions. Test what you know and read on to find out which Master you're most like... Maybe you'll uncover a darker layer lurking within yourself!

1. The Master has been the Doctor's frenemy on screen for over fifty years. In which episode are we first introduced to the character?

2. Over the years, the Master has teamed up with many a villain to help them take down the Doctor – or, worse, the universe! Which enemy did the Master ally with during 'Survival' (1989)?

A)   Cheetah People

B)   Cybermen

C)   The Nestene Consciouness

3. Which incarnation of the Master gave Clara Oswald the Doctor's phone number, in order to manipulate the pair into friendship?

4. The Master rarely cares about who or what they destroy, as long as they get to the Doctor. Which device does the Master use to compress the bodies of their victims, leaving a shrunken corpse behind as a miniature, doll-like structure?

A)   Tissue Compression Eliminator

B)   Miniaturisation Compressor

C)   Tissue Elimination Compressor

5. On what planet was the Master found during 'The Deadly Assassin' (1976), while in his final regeneration and near the end of his life?

A)   Earth

B)   Titan

C)   Tersurus

6. What name did the Master give himself when he became Prime Minister of the UK?

7. In which episode do the Time Lords offer the Master a new set of regenerations, if he will help them on their mission?

    A)   'The End of Time'

    B)   'The Five Doctors'

    C)   'The Three Doctors'

8. Over the years, we've had both multi-Doctor and multi-Master stories, always equalling chaos. How many incarnations of the Master appeared in 'World Enough and Time/The Doctor Falls' (2017)?

9. Out of the ones listed below, which incarnation of the Doctor *hasn't* met the Master on-screen?

    A)   The Ninth Doctor

    B)   The Third Doctor

    C)   The Seventh Doctor

A Familiar Face

Sacha Dhawan, who began playing the
Thirteenth Doctor's incarnation of the
Master in 2020, is no stranger to the
Whoniverse. The actor appeared in
An Adventure in Space and Time (2013),
a docu-drama celebrating the very
beginnings of *Doctor Who* – and played
Waris Hussein, the show's first Director.

10. Which creatures did the Master splice with Time Lord corpses to create a deadly new race in 'The Timeless Children' (2020)?

11. The Eighth Doctor met the Master after regenerating into his new body in the 1996 TV movie *Doctor Who*. Which actor played the Master during this adventure?

12. The Master has worked tirelessly to continue finding a form in which to keep living. Which companion's father did the Master assume the body and identity of in 'The Keeper of Traken' (1981)?

A) Nyssa's father

B) Tegan's father

C) Mel's father

13. Which type of screwdriver weapon does the Master reveal in 'The Sound of Drums', which only works with his DNA, leaving anybody else unable to use it?

14. Which organisation captured and imprisoned the Master on Earth, where he then attempted to help the Sea Devils rise up and take back the planet?

A) Torchwood

B) UNIT

C) MI5

15. Many brilliant actors have taken on the role of the Master. Who was the youngest actor to portray the Time Lord?

A) Sacha Dhawan

B) John Simm

C) William Hughes

Master Degree

The name 'Master' was chosen to be of
equal rank and importance to that
of the Doctor's name. It was thought
that the title should also be a form
of academic degree so that the two
characters were on a level playing field.
The two have battled it out over the years
to try and outrank each other — but their
origins and titles suggest more of an
equality between them.

Which Master Are You?

Every incarnation of the Master oozes evil.
They're mad, sociopathic and never give up on
their quest to hurt the Doctor. However, just like
the Doctor, every incarnation is unique; each
tackling their mission to conquer the universe a
little differently.

So, if you were a crazy, murderous Time Lord
whose sole mission was to get back at your old
friend – and maybe destroy some galaxies in
the process – which incarnation of the Master
would you be? Take the test below to find out …

**1. You want to get back at your frenemy the
Doctor by destroying their beloved Earth.
Which time period do you infiltrate to unfold
your plan?**

    A) Seventies London. The Doctor always
       seems to be lurking around that decade.
       Oh, and the fashion!

    B) The end of the universe. Nobody suspects
       you when you're using the far future to put
       an end to the past.

    C) You don't have a lot of choice in the

matter, as you've been stuck in a vault for almost 1,000 years.

D) You don't bother with a single period in time, you spread your plan throughout history to attempt to stop the Doctor foiling it.

2. You have to cunningly disguise yourself so that the Doctor and their friends will be unable to detect you. How do you choose to hide your identity?

A) You disguise yourself as whoever is necessary to create your murderous plot.

B) You fake your identity and pose as the prime minister.

C) You pretend to be an AI interface until the penny drops – your acting skills always fool the Doctor.

D) You assume the identity of someone who'll get the Doctor's attention and pretend to be their pal until your plan is underway.

3. Sometimes you have to let somebody else do the dirty work. So who do you team up with to take down the Doctor?

A) You ally with the Axos, a disgusting entity that will devour the Earth and all of the Doctor's silly friends – why lift a finger?

B) You create your own creatures out of humans from the future, and get them to murder half the population – that'll really upset the Doctor.

C) You team up with one of the Doctor's biggest enemies, the Cybermen, to do the hard bits – a great distraction for your bigger plan.

D) You use the Kasaavin to carry out your plan while you throw the Doctor off the scent.

4. You're alone with one of the Doctor's pesky friends and the temptation to get at your frenemy is too much to resist. Do you …

A) Respectfully and politely blackmail them to get to what you want.

B) Enslave them or their family to really get your message across.

C) Tie them up and taunt them – what fun!

D) Flirt with them – just in case it makes the Doctor jealous.

5. One day you'll be the ruler of the universe, so you must do everything in style. What attire do you wear to take down your enemies?

A) Something suave and black with gloves to portray your dark soul.

B) A suit to show your power and hold up your prime minister disguise.

C) A Mary Poppins-esque outfit with fabulous accessories. Why not go all out?

D) A waistcoat and bright socks – it has to be suitable if the whole universe is going to know your name.

6. You must be remembered as the Master of the universe. What iconic line will permanently embed you into your enemy's memories?

A) 'I am the Master and you will obey me.'

B) 'Here come the drums!'

C) 'Say something nice …'

D) 'Everything you think you know is a lie.'

7. The Doctor attempts to make amends and bring you over to their side. What do you do?

A) Repeatedly escape and figure out a new plan to take them down – it's quite fun, actually.

B) Let yourself die – you'd rather that than regenerate as it will hurt the Doctor more!

C) You give them a chance and stand alongside them – they are your friend, after all.

D) You taunt them with secrets of their past and destroy Gallifrey – you always knew the Doctor was different, and they deserve hell!

(Mostly As) The Original Master

Sociopathic yet polite, you're most like the original Master, who taunted the Third Doctor. You're happy to get others to do your dirty work and prefer to hypnotise your victims rather than manipulate them. You're calm and collected in the process – after all, you have full confidence in your plans. You tolerate and sometimes even work with your old pal the Doctor, keeping your frenemy close. It would be no fun without them around!

(Mostly Bs) The Saxon Master

You're most like the Saxon Master, who terrorised the Tenth and Twelfth Doctors. Bordering on insane and hell-bent on destroying the universe, you'll do anything to create the most horrifying plan possible. You're cruel, most of the time for fun, and hate the Doctor even more than your other regenerations. You will stop at nothing to cause them pain and destruction. Oh, and you should probably see someone about that drum beat in your head ...

(Mostly Cs) Missy

You're most like Master to the Twelfth Doctor, Missy. You're fun, fashionable and terribly evil, but can see why the Doctor might be in the right. You kill without guilt and destroy to get attention. You love to manipulate people and relationships, often playing the long game to get what you want. There's some good in there somewhere, though, and your friendship with the Doctor brings it out. Maybe you *can* be redeemed!

(Mostly Ds) The Spy Master

You're angry and you want revenge – just like the Spy Master, the Thirteenth Doctor's sworn enemy! You'll stop at nothing to get back at the Doctor now that you know the truth of who they really are. Obsessive, impulsive and full of rage, you'll kill anything that stands in your way, including your own people. You're ready to start a revolution to end things for good, and nobody could ever change your mind … You should probably get some help.

The Story That Never Was

The first incarnation of the Master, Roger Delgado, was originally supposed to appear in the Third Doctor's final story, where it would have been revealed that the characters were in fact siblings. Unfortunately, the beloved actor passed away in an accident in 1973 before the story could come to fruition and Jon Pertwee's final story was replaced with 'Planet of the Spiders'.

Chapter Eight

FUTURE TRAVELS

Adventuring with the Doctor means that we see wonders and, occasionally, the secrets of the future. From far-away starships to the end of the universe itself, we've witnessed the endless possibilities of what *could* be.

There's something incredibly fascinating about *Doctor Who* portraying how our future could go. Or guessing how we might spread across the stars and explore, showing us the planets and people we might find there. Beyond Earth, there's a vast cosmos filled with technological advances, space travel and potential. You may feel watching or reading those stories that this future potential is terrifying – the unknown isn't always comfortable. But for others, we might feel hope that if a future can be imagined, it can then be created and shaped into whatever we want it to be. That the world and our universe are far bigger than any of us, and we can impact where future generations might take us.

The real fun about hopping into the future with the Doctor and their pals is that anything can happen. Cat people and humans living together on a brand-new version of Earth! Robots that communicate via emojis! We've seen expansions in technology that we can currently only dream of, or might fear, such as artificial intelligence or cloning machines.

What's more exciting than watching our beloved blue box land on a futuristic planet or ship, where new ideas and adventures might abound?

There's a freedom in the future. If *Doctor Who* can dream it, then we create it: flying cars, brand-new planets, advanced travel. Some future TARDIS adventures have even taught us that there are some things we need to change, representing the impact of what will happen if we don't. We've stepped foot on faraway lands and learnt that the future might not be bright if things continue to stay the same. The Doctor may be giving us a wake-up call to make a change, because the future, of course, is down to us.

The past is fixed and certain, but the future is malleable. It is the place where *Doctor Who* can be the most radical or the most complex, because there is so much to explore. There's something for everyone when the TARDIS goes beyond our time, far into a future we haven't witnessed yet.

Are you a future fanatic? Travel to the end of the universe and back by testing your knowledge – you never know when you might need to imagine a better future ...

From the Future to the Past

Some *Who* stories were set in the future on broadcast, but now technically take place in the past. 'Fear Her' (2006) portrayed the events of the 2012 Olympic games, 1989's 'Battlefield' was set in 1997 and 2011's 'The Hungry Earth/Cold Blood' hopped to the near future of 2020. 'Fear Her' predicted one thing correctly – that the Doctor would carry the Olympic torch. Eleventh Doctor Matt Smith had a go at carrying the flame during the games, almost bringing part of the 2006 episode to life!

1. Many friends of the Doctor get to choose whether their first TARDIS trip is an adventure forward or backward in time. Which event does the Ninth Doctor take Rose Tyler to witness on her first trip into the future?

2. The consequences of travelling to the distant future can be disastrous. What does Dodo Chaplet infect the human and monoid races with, after she arrived on a generation starship with the First Doctor and Steven Taylor over ten million years into their future?

A)   A cold

B)   Chickenpox

C)   Coronavirus

3. The Eleventh Doctor took Amy Pond forward in time for her first TARDIS adventure, where they landed on *Starship UK*. Which creature powered the ship?

A)   The Lorax

B)   The Star Whale

C)   The Krafayis

4. The Doctor and their friends occasionally do not return from the future. In which story, set during the fifty-first century, did the Fifth Doctor regenerate?

5. Popping forward in time means the Doctor never knows who they might meet. On which planet did the Thirteenth Doctor and her 'Fam' meet the Dregs?

A)   Dreg Planet 55

B)   Orphan 57

C)   Orphan 55

6. Who did the Fourth Doctor meet when he travelled to the far future in 'The Face of Evil', who requested to travel with him on the TARDIS thereby becoming his new companion?

7. True or False? The Second Doctor and his friends met the Ice Warriors on the moon in the year 2089 during 'The Seeds of Death' (1969).

8. In 'Gridlock' (2007), the people of the City of New New York had died from an airborne virus, mutated from the mood drug 'Bliss'. Where were some of the population hidden and protected, unaware that the people above them had died out many years ago?

A)   The Motorway

B)   The Senate

C)   The Refugee Camp

9. Which First Doctor story was the first time *Doctor Who* ventured into the future?

A)   'The Ark'

B)   'The Keys of Marinus'

C)   'The Daleks'

10. In 'The Greatest Show in The Galaxy' (1988), the Seventh Doctor and Ace headed to the planet Segonax in the thirty-fifth century. To which circus on this planet were they invited?

A)   The Space Circus

B)   The Psychic Circus

C)   The Freak Show Circus

Future Ideas

The 1984 story 'Frontios' featured the insectoid Tractators. The story was originally supposed to integrate human body parts into the Tractator technology, but the idea was removed from the script. It was, however, later used in 2006's 'The Girl in the Fireplace', where the Clockwork Robots used human remains to power the technology aboard the SS *Madame de Pompadour*.

11. The Twelfth Doctor and Clara Oswald faced off against ghosts on an underwater base during which two-part story?

12. The future abounds with plenty of weird and wonderful creatures, robots and villains. 'The Happiness Patrol' featured the Kandyman, who appeared to be made up of which famous sweets?

A) Liquorice Allsorts

B) Jelly Babies

C) Fruit Pastilles

13. The Doctor and Rose Tyler met Lady Cassandra, who claimed to be the last 'pure' human, multiple times while adventuring in the future. Whose body did she eventually take over and die in, after leaving her framed skin form?

14. Which Doctor and companion landed on Varos in the twenty-third century, looking for rare mineral Zeiton-7 to fix the TARDIS?

15. The Third Doctor and Jo Grant found themselves in the twenty-sixth century during 'Frontier in Space'. Which race did they discover the Earth had been warring with?

A) The Dragons

B) The Draconians

C) The Daleks

16. Which retail warehouse did the Thirteenth Doctor and her friends visit, where robot delivery men were used to send packages to the humans that lived on Kandoka?

A) Kandoka Shopping PLC

B) Amazon

C) Kerb!am

The End of Everything

Many *Doctor Who* episodes have taken place in the far future, but the furthest the show has gone is the end of the universe itself! 'Utopia' (2007) portrayed humans and Futurekind living at the end of the universe, preparing to journey to a utopian planet for survival.

Later, in 2014's 'Listen', Orson Pink travelled to the end of time and space, and in 2015's 'Hell Bent', the Twelfth Doctor finds immortal 'Me' watching the stars and planets fade out from Gallifrey using a reality bubble.

Find the Future

If you're a fan of looking ahead, adventure through this time-wimey wordsearch to find words from futuristic *Doctor Who*. From colonies on Mars to the end of the universe, can you find all of these TARDIS adventures, friends and enemies from the future?

Futurekind

Kerblam

Monoids

End of the World

Emojibots

Planet of Evil

Draconians

Face of Boe

Leela

Dragonfire

Sil

Nardole

D	E	N	D	O	F	T	H	E	W	O	R	L	D
R	M	E	M	O	J	I	B	O	T	S	R	N	I
A	F	B	S	D	N	A	R	D	O	L	E	F	I
G	M	A	D	N	I	K	E	R	U	T	U	F	O
O	N	M	C	O	E	I	O	L	I	E	A	E	T
N	I	O	I	E	P	D	L	O	E	P	S	I	L
F	E	N	F	R	O	R	U	A	R	E	C	O	H
I	B	O	O	N	B	F	I	E	W	L	L	A	I
R	B	I	D	O	R	A	B	L	I	N	N	A	O
E	O	D	L	E	F	A	I	O	H	M	N	I	S
D	B	S	L	D	N	L	R	R	E	A	T	G	R
K	E	R	B	L	A	M	D	B	F	L	U	R	E
L	I	V	E	F	O	T	E	N	A	L	P	D	T
F	S	N	A	I	N	O	C	A	R	D	W	N	T

Chapter Nine

THE CYBERMEN

With their blank eyes, emotionless voice and creepy humanoid appearance, the Cybermen are enough to send a chill down any spine. These pesky Cyber threats have been terrorising the Doctor (and the universe) for almost as long as the Daleks, making them equally iconic.

The creatures inside a Cyber suit used to be people before they had every aspect of their humanity stripped away. Every emotion, every memory and every reaction was removed, the shell that is left becoming a vessel to house a new race of heartless monsters.

The history of the Cybermen is complex and there are many origin stories of the giant metal men. They are the apparent next step in our evolution – if humans are dying out, why not upgrade to something better? Remove pain and put what remains of us into the ultimate suit of survival! This has resulted in multiple types of Cybermen originating from different worlds and universes – all beginning as people, ready to evolve. We never know where they'll appear next, in what form or how they will have changed. The unknown and unpredictability can raise fear in us just as much as their scary appearance.

Some of the best Cybermen moments have come from when they're faced with their own brutality: conversion has failed and they can feel pain, despite their reformed existence. The thing that makes them so terrifying is their closeness to us, but their ability to also be nothing like us. They're 'upgraded' versions of a thinking, feeling and living being, and there's nothing more horrifying than not being able to feel at all.

When you think of the Cybermen, you might think of their famous menacing walk down the steps of St Paul's. Or you might be reminded of the Battle of Canary Wharf, where they finally met their match against the Daleks. Maybe you're a Mondasian fan or dig the speedy Cybies from 'Nightmare in Silver'? Whatever part of their history you prefer, there's a space behind the sofa for every Cyberman moment.

Think you know your Cybershades from your Cyber-mats? Your Cyber-Controller from your Cyber-Leader? This chapter will test your knowledge and prepare you for conversion, should you ever end up at the mercy of a Cyberman ...

1. What year did the Cybermen first debut in *Doctor Who*, during William Hartnell's final episode as the First Doctor 'The Tenth Planet'?

2. Every enemy of the Doctor has a weakness. What material are some versions of the Cybermen allergic to?

3. Which companion was converted into a Cyberman after getting shot during 'World Enough and Time/The Doctor Falls' (2017)?

    A)   Bill Potts

    B)   Nardole

    C)   Clara Oswald

4. True or False? Two people came up with the idea of the Cybermen – Dr Kit Pedler, a scientific advisor for *Doctor Who*, and Gerry Davis, the show's story editor.

5. There are many different types and ranks of Cybermen. A Cyberman with black handles on its helmet is commonly known as what?

Cyber Origins

Surgery to replace failing organs and parts of the body experienced rapid development in medicine during the 1960s. Dr Kit Pedler had the idea for the Cybermen after a discussion with his wife. They spoke about the possibilities of a person having so many artificial replacements added to their bodies that they would become more machine than human. The result of this conversation was the creation of one of the Doctor's most haunting enemies.

6. Which planet was home to a tomb chock-full of Cybermen in 'The Tomb of the Cybermen' (1967)?

A) Mondas

B) Atrapos

C) Telos

D) Tralpos

7. The head of a Cyberman became the Doctor's companion while he was protecting the planet Trenzalore during 'The Time of the Doctor'. What name did he give to his Cyber friend?

8. What device, fitted into a Cyberman suit, stops them from feeling emotions such as love, fear or pain?

A) The Emotion Stopper

B) The Emotional Inhibitor

C) The Emotion Matrix

9. Cybermats acted as agents for the Cybermen, used for sabotage or to do their dirty work for them. Which insect inspired their design?

A)   Ladybird

B)   Beetle

C)   Wood lice

10. When the Cybermen returned to *Doctor Who* in 2006, they came with a terrifying new catchphrase. What was their murderous cry before they took down their victims?

Cyber Designer

The very first Cybermen were made by costume designer Sandra Reid, who then redesigned them for 1967's 'The Moonbase'. These designs have lived on in various forms over the years, with Sandra's original concept even being updated and brought back for 'World Enough and Time/The Doctor Falls' (2017). Reid also contributed to the realising of the Second Doctor's iconic outfit.

11. Which Doctor battled the Cybermen on *Space Station Nerva*, where the silver villains spread a fatal infection to the crew of the ship in an attempt to wipe them out and destroy the planet Voga?

A)   The Fourth Doctor

B)   The Fifth Doctor

C)   The Sixth Doctor

D)   The Seventh Doctor

12. Cybermen are all about upgrading. In which story did we first see that the Cybermen had gained the ability to fly?

A)   'Ascension of the Cybermen/The Timeless Children'

B)   'Dark Water/Death in Heaven'

C)   'Rise of the Cybermen/Age of Steel'

13. Which comedian and talk show host played Craig Owens – the Doctor's friend who rejected conversion to become a Cyberman during 2011's 'Closing Time', because he was overwhelmed with love for his son?

14. True or False? Henry van Statten kept a Cyberman helmet in his museum, much to the Doctor's surprise when he and Rose Tyler arrived there in 'Dalek'.

15. What did Ashad (The Lone Cyberman) chase through time that would enable him to re-build the Cyber-Empire, which he eventually obtained from the hands of the Thirteenth Doctor in 'The Haunting of Villa Diodati' (2020)?

   A) The Cyberium

   B) The Cyberiad

   C) The Cyberio

Cyber Match

The Cyberman databases have been corrupted and you're the only Cyber scout left that can fix the damage. Match the Cyber episodes to the year they aired to fix the database and put the Cybermen back on track with their newest deadly mission …

The Next Doctor

2020

Rise of the Cybermen/The Age of Steel

Revenge of the Cybermen

2006

1985

2013

The Tenth Planet

The Tomb of the Cybermen

2014

Nightmare in Silver

1975

Attack of the Cybermen

Ascension of the Cybermen/The Timeless Children

2008

1967

Dark Water/Death in Heaven

1966

Doctors Who Didn't Meet the Cybermen

The Third, Eighth and Ninth Doctors are the only full-time incarnations of our hero that didn't war with the Cybermen on-screen. The metal men were absent for the entirety of the Third Doctor's era and didn't return until they faced off with the Fourth Doctor, in 'Revenge of the Cybermen' (1975). They failed to make an appearance in the 1996 TV Movie *Doctor Who* or any episode of the Ninth Doctor's only series. However, all three incarnations have encountered the Cybermen in Big Finish audio dramas.

Chapter Ten

FRIENDS OF THE DOCTOR, PART TWO

There's something to love in every TARDIS traveller: Jo Grant and her loyalty, Bill Potts and her questions, Rory Williams and his humour. They are friends that hold our hands through time and space, who we wish we could pull right out of the TV and into our own lives. Who wouldn't want to gossip over a cuppa with Rose Tyler, or chat history with Barbara Wright?

You might know them as well as your friends, too – their hopes, their dreams, their fears, where they came from and where they're going. Their wonderful travels in the TARDIS are held in our hearts for ever. Let's jump straight aboard the TARDIS to celebrate our love for the Doctor's friends by answering the following. Which companion ...

A: Was given their TARDIS Key in 'Aliens of London'?

B: Died while trying to change the course of a freighter heading towards Earth?

C: Had a favourite cat named Biggles?

D: Attended Coal Hill School as a student?

E: Walked the Earth to save the Doctor, and the world, from the Master?

F: Originally came from Victorian England?

G: Guarded the Pandorica for nearly 2,000 years?

H: First appeared in 'Planet of Fire'?

I: Shot a Dalek with a paintball gun?

J: Was the Doctor's laboratory assistant?

K: Attended lectures by the Doctor before being personally tutored by him?

1. The Third Doctor had many friends at UNIT, including scientist Liz Shaw. How many stories did she appear in?

A) Six

B) Four

C) One

2. What name is given to a trio of the Doctor's friends consisting of Madame Vastra, Strax the Sontaran and Jenny Flint?

3. Throughout the years, we've encountered four versions of robot dog K9. Who originally built the Doctor's trusty friend?

A) Professor Marius

B) The Third Doctor

C) Professor J Smith

4. How did Ian Chesterton and Barbara Wright return home to their own time in the sixties, after travelling with the First Doctor?

A) Through a wormhole

B) By TARDIS

C) Via a Dalek time ship

5. Which companion of the Doctor convinced the first incarnation of our hero which TARDIS to steal, way back when he was about to leave Gallifrey?

6. Which friends of the Second Doctor had their minds wiped before being sent back to their own time, left only able to remember their first encounter with the Doctor?

7. The Doctor had a fan and a firm friend in Osgood. What is the UNIT scientific advisor's first name?

A) Perpugilliam

B) Petronella

C) Petunia

8. Which creatures did Ben Jackson and Polly Wright encounter on their final adventure with the Doctor?

A) The Chameleons

B) The Quarks

C) The Macra

9. Nardole was the Twelfth Doctor's friend and companion, who joined him and Bill Potts for some TARDIS adventures. Which UK comedian played the cyborg?

10. Many of the Doctor's friends have met multiple incarnations of the Time Lord. In which episode did the Doctor's long-time friend 'The Brigadier' first appear?

A) 'Spearhead from Space'

B) 'The Web of Fear'

C) 'The Invasion'

11. Which friend of the Tenth Doctor decided to stay and live in a parallel world, after realising there was more of a life for him there?

Companions That Never Were

Some companions never made it aboard the TARDIS due to production changes or re-writes. Ray, who met the Seventh Doctor in 'Delta and the Bannermen' (1987), was originally supposed to take over as companion after the departure of Mel Bush, but was replaced by Ace. Tenth Doctor companion Donna Noble was nearly Penny, a brand-new character who would have been cast, had Catherine Tate turned down the offer to return to *Doctor Who*. Fortunately for us, the rest was history!

12. The Doctor makes friends wherever they travel. Which planet did companion to the Fourth and Fifth Doctors, Nyssa, originate from?

A) Traken

B) Gallifrey

C) Clom

13. True or False? Companion to the Fourth Doctor Harry Sullivan was never seen inside the TARDIS on-screen while travelling with the Doctor and Sarah Jane Smith.

14. Which Doctor's regeneration did Grace Holloway accidentally commence, after trying to perform surgery on him when he was shot by a gang outside his TARDIS?

15. The Doctor's friends are constantly being used as tools to get to the Doctor and, by extent, cause chaos and destruction. Which creature possessed Tegan Jovanka, during 1983's 'Snakedance'?

A) The Great Snake

B) The Mara

C) The Mirror

The Youngest Companion

The Doctor's companions vary in age, with a trend of friends in their late teens/early twenties boarding the TARDIS. Victoria Waterfield was around fourteen years old when she first joined for adventures. After losing her father to the Daleks, the Second Doctor and Jamie took her under their wing at the request of her late dad, making her the youngest friend to become a companion on the show.

Who Almost Made It?

The Doctor makes friends wherever they end up, with the lucky few offered a trip of a lifetime. There have been many brilliant people that have almost become the Doctor's companion over the years, but never quite got their adventure in the TARDIS. Some turned down the offer, some asked and were refused, and others lost their lives before getting the chance to see the universe. We rooted for them, we fell in love with them, and grieved the ones lost too soon. Sometimes, we might have even seen ourselves in them, as we wait for our own moment to travel the stars. Despite their short-lived friendships or adventures with the Doctor, we still cared for them as if they were a permanent TARDIS resident.

Can you name the companions who never were? Do you remember their hopes, their almosts and their losses? Test what you know about these brilliant friends overleaf.

Who ...?

1. Fell in love with a human version of the Doctor but declined to travel with him once he had become his Time Lord self again?

2. Helped the Doctor defeat the Foretold but decided not to travel aboard the TARDIS for fear that engineering such a ship could 'change a man'?

3. Became companion to the Doctor aboard a spaceship named *Titanic* but sacrificed herself to kill Max Capricorn before getting the chance to leave for adventures on the TARDIS?

4. Helped the Doctor defeat the Master and the Kasaavin alongside Noor Inayat Khan and begged the Doctor to take her travelling – only to have her mind wiped of the adventures she'd had?

5. Was refused by the Doctor to travel aboard the TARDIS because he did not want to travel with a soldier?

7. Was brutally killed by the Minotaur aboard a prison ship disguised as a hotel before getting the chance to take the Doctor up on his offer to travel with him?

8. Asked the Doctor if she could travel with him after meeting aboard the Game Station, but was exterminated by the Daleks before she could join the TARDIS?

The Constant Companion

Clara Oswald met the most incarnations of the Doctor, after jumping into their time stream to save them from the Great Intelligence. She split into various versions of herself and met all eleven incarnations up to that point, as well as the War Doctor. She then helped the Doctor through his regeneration to their Twelfth incarnation, travelling with him before leaving the TARDIS in 2015.

Chapter Eleven

EARTH INVASIONS

Whether they're looking for a new home or want to utilise our natural resources, aliens and villains from around the universe are always picking our bountiful planet for invasion. Luckily, the Doctor also happens to adore us and our world, serving as our protector against those who invade from the stars. There may be damage left in their wake, but the Doctor and their friends are always on hand to thwart an Earth-ending plan.

Earth invasions in *Doctor Who* reflect some of the harsher sides of our world and how we respond to them. When we are threatened, do we respond out of fear? How do we react when an alien race needs a new home? How can we right now do better, to avoid conflict, war and pain? Watching soldiers shoot at innocent creatures, or ships being shot down as they leave the Earth, perhaps reflects how it's almost human nature to respond out of fear. Sometimes it is natural to react without contemplating the full picture, making a situation worse or hurting others without meaning to. Perhaps we have learnt from the Doctor that, when faced with something new or scary, we should take the kindest and fairest route to deal with it.

It is also more terrifying to witness aliens in our own cities and homes than on spaceships or faraway worlds. We've seen Daleks menacing their way across Westminster Bridge and Sontarans taking over the streets of Liverpool. What's to say there isn't some monster hidden away in your town, hatching a plan to destroy humanity? We are equally fascinated and scared of *Doctor Who* when the threat might directly affect us and our lives.

These invasions also show us that adventure can happen right where we are. Life can be full of surprises, threats to defeat and friends to be made in the process. Even if we aren't facing the Slitheen or Weeping Angels today, we might be facing something tomorrow – and the Doctor is always there to protect us or show us how to protect ourselves. We can have adventures and see wonders on our doorstep and still be home in time for tea.

Did you witness The Battle of Canary Wharf? Have you heard the fables of when the Yeti terrorised the underground? Find out how much you know with these Earth invasion questions – after all, you never know when you might need to defend your home planet on behalf of the Doctor...

Invasion of the Really Great Sets

'The Web of Fear' (1968) featured the terrifying robot Yeti haunting the London Underground. The sets were apparently so accurate and realistic that the BBC received a complaint from London Transport – who thought that filming had taken place on the actual London Underground, without their permission!

1. Why did the Saturnyns want to flood sixteenth-century Venice and kidnap female inhabitants of the city?

2. What villains attempted to take over and control the human race via a signal sent out through International Electromatics devices?

3. Which countries did the Sontarans invade when they infiltrated history, renaming them after their home planet, 'Sontar'?

4. Which cyborg sea creature did the Zygons use as a weapon in an attempt to help them take over the Earth?

5. What is the name of the Earth space probe that the Sycorax followed to our planet, causing them to launch an invasion and attempt to enslave humanity?

6. How did a Rutan creature come to be on Earth in 1902, where it terrorised the inhabitants of Fang Rock?

7. How long had Cyber ghosts been appearing regularly on Earth, before the Doctor and Rose Tyler landed in London and discovered the mystery?

    A)   Three months

    B)   Six months

    C)   Two months

8. Why were the Daleks drilling to the core of the Earth when they invaded in the middle of the twenty-second century?

9. The family Slitheen came to Earth in 'Aliens of London/World War Three' (2005), hoping to start World War III and sell pieces of our destroyed planet for profit. What chemical element are their bodies made up of?

10. How did the Kraals plan to wipe out the people of Earth, leaving the planet clear for colonisation?

Entirely Earth-Bound Seasons

Some seasons of *Doctor Who* were set almost exclusively on Earth. The Third Doctor's first season (Season 7) and the Seventh Doctor's final season (Season 26) were entirely Earth-based stories, aside from a parallel universe in 'Inferno' (1970) and a trip to the planet of the Cheetah People in 'Survival' (1989).

Series 1 of New *Who* also didn't stray further than the Earth's orbit, where the Ninth Doctor and Rose visited Satellite Five – with every other story taking place on our soil.

11. How many times have the Nestene Consciousness attempted to take over the Earth?

12. The Boneless came to our planet from a universe where dimensions work differently. What differs between their universe and our own?

13. What London Underground station did the Doctor, Jamie and Victoria land in before discovering the terrifying Yeti had invaded the system?

A) Covent Garden

B) High Barnet

C) Leicester Square

14. Which creatures used a virtually simulated reality of planet Earth in order to plan an invasion and take control of the human race?

15. In which episode do the Doctor and their friends experience the 'Year of the Slow Invasion'?

Earth Invaders or Inhabitants?

Some alien creatures were here before us, or even form a part of our planet ... According to 'The Runaway Bride' (2006), the Earth owes its existence to the Racnoss, an ancient, arachnid-like race whose *Webstar* ship was the core around which our planet formed, and in 'Kill the Moon' (2014) it was revealed that our moon is actually a giant alien egg! Other creatures such as the Silurians and Sea Devils originally inhabited our planet before the human race came to be.

Name that Invasion!

We all have an Earth Invasion that haunts our dreams … Can you remember the Christmas the Racnoss came? Or do you live in fear of the return of the Daleks?

How well do you remember the aliens that flew above our cities or threatened our world? Jump back into invasions of the Earth and find out how much you know by naming the invasion episode based on the clues. You'll need to keep a record, just in case any enemies decide to return …

Question	Clue	Answer
1	Snow. Gas. Wales. Author.	
2	Moon. Rocket. Solar. Ice.	
3	Silver. Royal. Comet. Cyber.	

Question	Clue	Answer
4	Chips. School. Oil.	
5	Plastic Dummies. Exile. Regeneration.	
6	Painting. Trafalgar Square. No More.	
7	Simulation. Control. Monk.	
8	Scotland. Oil. Duplicate.	
9	Downing Street. Big Ben. Pig.	
10	Crash-landing. Middle Ages. Warrior.	

Chapter Twelve

PLANETS & WORLDS

Sometimes we just need to escape to a different world and *Doctor Who* gives us exactly that opportunity. There are planets to explore, civilisations to meet and new lessons to learn – when the TARDIS lands on fresh soil, we're always in for an exciting ride.

Something that makes *Who* so special is its creation of a universe that we want to come back to repeatedly spend time in. Over the past six decades, galaxies and worlds have been built to create a place that we can run away to and cheer ourselves up with. Whether it's Earth, on Gallifrey, Midnight or Skaro, there's an endless list of planets to land on.

There's something extra special about being able to traverse new worlds from our own homes. Whether we're visiting the Ood Sphere, Traken or Cheetah World, alien skies and beautiful landscapes await. Each new TARDIS landing spot and the Doctor's discovery of wonders helps us to see the beauty in our own lives. It may be not apple grass, skies made of diamonds or mountains that move, but we have just as much to see out in our local parks, beaches and forests. Sometimes, walking across alien sand with the Doctor brings us that sense of adventure that we've been looking for to get out and explore our own world.

Perhaps exploring these worlds comforts us and helps us to realise that we are not alone. After all, we have the Doctor, their friends and countless planets to visit.

Or each adventure might allow us to realise our love for travel and take it up in our real lives. How many of us have travelled around the country for a *Doctor Who* event or meet-up? Or decided to visit somewhere new because the show revealed that it was possible? That's what the *Doctor Who* universe inspires, the idea that we can go anywhere, wherever we like, real or imagined.

We could fly to New Earth with the Tenth Doctor and Rose, or visit Marinus with the First Doctor, Ian, Barbara and Susan. We can revisit our favourite galaxies whenever we like with the Doctor. Looking out beyond the stars, we can imagine and live in a universe much bigger than ourselves – and what is more hopeful than that?

So, grab a scarf and some sunglasses (because you never know where you'll end up) and board the TARDIS for an adventure through the galaxies by testing what you know about planets and worlds in *Doctor Who*. It's always good to be prepared, in case you end up caught up in a time storm … Get kidnapped by aliens … Or if a strange blue box appears in your living room …

Ood in Wales

Scenes for the Ood Sphere, the icy planet
seen in 2008's 'Planet of the Ood',
were filmed during a hot summer in 2007.
To create the snowy landscape, tiny pieces
of paper were used to make fake snow,
paired with CGI. The scenes were
filmed in a quarry in the Brecon Beacons,
which turned out to be the perfect
landscape upon which to create the
Ood planet!

1. What is the twin planet of Clom?

2. Which creature did the Doctor befriend on Peladon, whose almost extinct species were usually found living in the mountains of the planet?

3. Which prison planet are Daleks sent to when they malfunction or go insane?

4. On which planet did the First Doctor meet his companion, Vicki?

5. The Thirteenth Doctor and her friends got caught up in which racing competition on the planet Desolation?

    A)   The Galaxy Race

    B)   The Rally of the Twelve Galaxies

    C)   The Desolation Race

6. Mars has frequently appeared in *Doctor Who*. Which 'Eye' was kept in a Pyramid on Mars?

7. The Doctor and River Song shared their final date on the planet Darillium. How long does a night last on the planet?

8. Gallifrey, Draconia, Sontar and Earth all reside in which Time Lord named Galaxy?

    A)   Milker Galaxy

    B)   Mutter's Spiral

    C)   Andromeda

9. The Ninth Doctor and Rose Tyler visited Woman Wept, which was given its namesake from its continent shaped like a lamenting woman. Who stole this planet and placed it in the Medusa Cascade?

10. Fifth Doctor companion Turlough was exiled from his home planet Trion for what reason?

11. In which nebula were both the Ood Sphere and the Sense Sphere located?

12. The Seventh Doctor and Ace ended up on Cheetah Planet in 'Survival' – what was special about this planet?

    A) It had no moon

    B) It was made of ice

    C) It was sentient

13. Which church sought to protect the planet Trenzalore from being destroyed and stop the Time Lords from returning through a crack in time?

14. Which race lived on Telos before the Cybermen colonised the planet and murdered most of the native inhabitants?

15. The Doctor and Rose Tyler landed on Krop Tor, where they faced a terrifying black hole, possessed Ood and 'The Beast'. What name does Krop Tor translate to?

16. Upon the Daleks' home planet, Skaro, there is a deadly lake of...

    A)   Mutations

    B)   Kaleds

    C)   Toxic waste

17. Which planet is also known as 'The Web Planet'?

World of Ratings

The first episode of one of *Doctor Who*'s earliest ventures to an alien planet, 'The Web Planet' (1965), had the highest number of viewers than any other single *Who* episode in the sixties. The entire story, famous for featuring giant ant-like creatures the Zarbi, also had the collected highest average viewing figure for the entire First Doctor era, at 13.5 million viewers.

Which World?

The TARDIS databanks have been corrupted by an alien virus, deleting vital information and records of the Doctor's adventures. Can you fill in the gaps and update the database by answering which planet each of the characters below originated from?

You must be quick, before the files are erased…

1. The Thals ....

2. Astrid Peth ....

3. Chantho ....

4. Adric ....

5. The Sensorites ....

6. Prentis ....

7. Erato ....

8. The Mouri ....

9. The Drahvins ....

10. The Thijarians ....

Location, Location, Location

The Canary Islands have been home to many a planet in *Doctor Who*. 'Planet of Fire' (1984) featured Lanzarote as the planet Sarn and the show returned to the island in 2014 to create the surface of the moon in 'Kill the Moon'. Series 9 of New *Who* (2015) featured scenes filmed in Tenerife for a Skaro landscape in 'The Magician's Apprentice/The Witch's Familiar', and Fuerteventura doubled for Gallifrey in 'Heaven Sent/Hell Bent'. That's a lot of sandy landscapes!

Chapter Thirteen

DEFENDERS OF
THE EARTH

Whether you're a fan of the UNIT era of *Doctor Who*, grew up on Bannerman Road with *The Sarah Jane Adventures*, or love the gritty spin-off *Torchwood*, the Doctor's Earth defenders offer something for everyone. Maybe you came of age with the *Class* gang, or now spend your commute listening to the 'Blue Box Files' girls in *Doctor Who: Redacted*. Whichever is your favourite, you'll always find a bit of the Doctor here on Earth, whether they're walking our planet or flying through the outer reaches of the universe.

We've watched companions such as Sarah Jane Smith and Martha Jones return home and help thwart invasions. We've listened as a trio of best friends managed to stop the Doctor and the planet's population from being completely redacted. Friends of the Doctor have helped to stop the Daleks from using their reality bomb and have halted the Trickster in his tracks. They've been here on Earth when the Doctor hasn't, taking us on adventures outside of the TARDIS. Not only have these friends and allies been left in charge when the Doctor is not around, but they often team up with our hero to conquer evil. Even a Time Lord needs a helping hand and that's what these characters and spin-off shows bring to the *Doctor Who* universe.

It is something of a comfort knowing how many of the Doctor's friends are there for us. We can imagine them fighting our corner and be inspired by their bravery. They teach us that we can also step up and fight, just in case our favourite Time Lord isn't around to help out. We watch the Doctor save the world and learn how to do so ourselves: from tackling climate change to deciding the best people to lead us, we also do our bit. We can be the Kate Stewart or the Captain Jack Harkness of our patch of Earth, making a difference one step at a time.

This chapter of quizzes celebrates some of our favourite Earth protectors, as well as their adventures, friends and enemies: Sarah Jane and her Bannerman Road gang, Torchwood, UNIT, the Coal Hill students who defended the Earth in *Class* and the Doctor's friends from *Redacted*. How well do you know the teams and organisations that assist the Doctor in saving us time and time again? Find out by tackling these tricky questions and see if you have what it takes to be an Earth defender!

1. How many incarnations of the Doctor have the Brigadier and his daughter, Kate Stewart, collectively met?

2. In which year was the Torchwood Institute founded?

3. The Bane artificially created a boy who later went on to become Sarah Jane Smith's adopted son, Luke. What name did the Bane give to their creation?

4. What caused a tear in space and time around Coal Hill School, leading a band of students to team up to protect the area from alien forces?

5. Where did the Master, disguised as Harold Saxon, send the Torchwood Three gang on a wild goose chase mission during the events of 'The Sound of Drums' (2007)?

The Almost Spin-Off

When the BBC was looking to commission a children's *Doctor Who* spin-off, the initial idea was for a drama series based around a younger version of the Doctor. Showrunner Russell T Davies wasn't happy with the idea though, stating, 'Somehow, the idea of a fourteen-year-old Doctor, on Gallifrey, inventing sonic screwdrivers, takes away from the mystery and intrigue of who he is and where he came from.' Instead, he suggested a series based on Sarah Jane Smith – thus, *The Sarah Jane Adventures* was born!

6. Which podcast aimed to uncover the mystery of the Doctor and their blue box?

7. Two members of which Raxacoricofallapatorian family gifted deadly Rakweed to Sarah Jane and her gang in an attempt to cover the Earth with the plant and sell it off for profit?

8. Where was Torchwood Two based?

9. Which incident did the Tenth Doctor save Cleo Proctor from, which also resulted in the death of Cleo's father?

10. Coal Hill student Charlie Smith was the alien prince of which planet?

11. UNIT was founded in the late 1960s. Which extra-terrestrial incident did they miss and was one of the many reasons Alistair Lethbridge-Stewart was brought into UNIT?

12. Which alien creature was Torchwood member Toshiko Sato sent to London to investigate in 2006?

13. In which *The Sarah Jane Adventures* story does everybody turn against Clyde Langer, leaving him homeless on the streets of London?

14. Which Coal Hill student shared a heart with Corakinus, king of the deadly Shadow Kin?

15. The Seventh Doctor and Ace met Winifred Bambera in the late nineties. What rank did she hold while working at UNIT during this time?

16. Which companion of the Doctor has worked for both UNIT and Torchwood?

Torchwood Tapes

The idea for the name of spin-off *Torchwood* came after TV pirates were eager to get hold of *Doctor Who* tapes during production of the early series of New *Who*. Someone suggested labelling the tapes as 'Torchwood' instead of *Doctor Who* so that the contents remained a mystery. Russell T Davies loved the idea so much that he used it for a more adult *Who* spin-off drama.

The Black Archive: Memory Mayhem

Can you remember your *Class* episodes from your UNIT stories? Your Sarah Jane adventures from your *Torchwood* escapades? Dive into the Black Archive and complete the episode titles below to test your knowledge. You'll need to remember these incidents in case you ever take over the role of protecting the Earth from an alien threat …

A) ___ _____ We Might Die
B) The _____ Death
C) ____ Man Walking
D) _____ _____ to Sarah Jane?
E) _____ __ ___ Dinosaurs
F) The _____ _____, or What Quill Did
G) ____ Wounds
H) Mona Lisa's _____
I) The Power __ _____
J) ___ __ the Gorgon
K) Redacted: S_____
L) ____ Left
M) Secrets __ ___ _____
N) ___ ____ _____ Suzie
O) _____-__ Heart

UNIT Association

During the classic series of *Doctor Who*, UNIT initially stood for the 'United Nations Intelligence Taskforce'. When the show came back in 2005, the UN chose not to be associated with *Doctor Who* any longer and asked for the name to be changed or removed, leaving the production team only able to call the organisation UNIT. When UNIT appeared in Series 4 (2008), the full name had been changed to the 'Unified Intelligence Taskforce'.

Chapter Fourteen

GALLIFREY & THE
TIME LORDS

The Doctor is a Time Lord from Gallifrey who stole a TARDIS and ran away. Or are they?

According to 'The Timeless Children' (2020), the Doctor may not actually be from Gallifrey at all, but a lost child found by a Gallifreyan on another world. Ultimately, wherever the Doctor was born, they grew up on the orange planet with its burning skies and silver-leaved trees. They eventually left the mountains and the Capitol of Gallifrey to adventure the universe and the Time Lords have been attempting to stop them ever since.

The Doctor – and by extension, the audience – have a complicated relationship with the Time Lords. After all, they haven't always been heroic or kind. They are the rulers of all of time and space, which makes them a complex bunch. At times, they've used their abilities to abuse other species, even destroying countless civilisations in their war against the Daleks. They've experimented on the Doctor, exiled them to Earth and even trapped them in a confession dial. To some, the Time Lords might be exactly what the Doctor was running from: a place they didn't fit and perhaps even feared.

The story of a lone wolf leaving their home behind is one that might resonate with lots of us. Maybe it is why we relate to the Doctor so much – if your own home or situation has been a place of hurt, you too would want to run away from them. Despite our kinship to where our roots are, the Doctor's relationship with Gallifrey and its people shows us that it is okay to choose our own path and find where we belong. Whether that's a faraway place or somewhere our real friends may be, there's more for us out there than what we were born into.

The Time Lords also give us a different perspective on the universe aside from our own planet. They are ancient lords of the universe, who may seem similar to our race but are really so far away from anything we could fathom. What would we become if we were given the chance to control the stars? This may be our lesson: to never interfere with the universe around us, unless with kindness and a good heart.

This chapter covers all things Gallifreyan. Whether you're a firm fan of the rulers of the universe, or fear their power, you'll find their history detailed in these pages to test yourself on. So, how well do you know the history of the Time Lords?

Mysterious Planet

Gallifrey was portrayed on screen before the planet was even given a name. It first appeared in 'The War Games' (1969) and then later in 'The Three Doctors' (1972), but wasn't actually named until 1973's 'The Time Warrior'!

1. Home to the Time Lords, the planet Gallifrey resides in which constellation?

2. Which game used the 'Death Zone' on Gallifrey?

3. What instigated the Eighth Doctor's regeneration into the War Doctor, a face they chose to help them take on the Time War?

4. What are the indigenous people of Gallifrey called?

5. The Hand of Omega transformed stars into supernovas in order to fuel what?

6. Where was the Doctor found as a child by Tecteun?

7. In which story do the Time Lords grant the Doctor a new regeneration cycle?

8. Who played Rassilon in 'The End of Time' (2009)?

9. Gallifrey is integral to the Doctor's journey, but has only appeared a handful of times over the years. In which story did the planet first appear?

10. Where does a Time Lord mind go when it dies?

11. Which bell can be found not only in a TARDIS, but also upon Gallifrey, which usually sounds during times of danger?

12. Why did the Time Lords exile the Doctor to Earth?

13. Name the two alien races that invaded Gallifrey during 'The Invasion of Time' (1978).

14. Which character was the first Time Lord to appear in *Doctor Who*, aside from the Doctor and Susan Foreman?

15. Gallifrey is vast and beautiful, with orange skies and snow-capped mountains. On which continent of Gallifrey was the Capitol located?

Time Lords and Ladies

Confirmation that Time Lords were able to regenerate into different genders came in 2011's 'The Doctor's Wife', when the Eleventh Doctor explained that fellow Time Lord, the Corsair, was a man but had before been a woman. In 2014, the Master regenerated into Missy (first seen in 'Deep Breath') and, in 2017, Jodie Whittaker was announced to take over the reins of the TARDIS as the first female Doctor.

The Crossword of Rassilon

If you fancy yourself a Time Lord of Gallifrey, look no further for the ultimate test. Complete the crossword of Rassilon and initiate yourself into Gallifreyan history...

ACROSS

3. Where young Time Lord initiation happens
4. Creatures found beneath the Capitol
6. Caregiver to the Timeless Child
7. A weapon with a friendly face
8. A place from which artron energy comes
10. Time Lord judge
11. Six-sided room in the Capitol
12. A founder of Time Lord civilisation
14. The last will and testament of a Time Lord
16. Orange and red Time Lord chapter
19. The Time Lords vs the Daleks

DOWN

1. Gallifrey's second city
2. A link used by the Master to bring Gallifrey back through the immortality gate
5. Story that introduced Rassilon and Borusa
6. Renegade Time Lady
9. Gallifreyan communication box

13. A mountain on Gallifrey where the Citadel Resides
15. Gallifrey Falls
17. Assisted the Doctor in the quest to find the Key to Time
18. Scientist who enabled Gallifreyan time travel

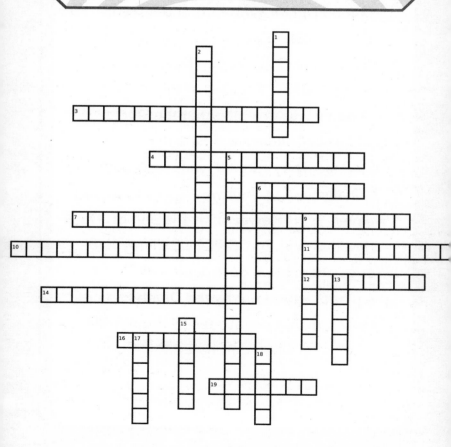

The Destruction of Gallifrey

When *Doctor Who* returned in 2005 after almost 16 years off air, the Doctor believed that Gallifrey had been destroyed – until 2013's 'The Day of the Doctor', when it was revealed that the Doctor could save Gallifrey and hide it in a pocket universe. They spent a while looking for it, finally finding their way back in 2015's 'Heaven Sent'. However, by the end of 'The Timeless Children' (2020), Gallifrey had once again been destroyed – all life on the planet wiped out by the Death Particle, a weapon that devastates all organic life when detonated.

Chapter Fifteen

BEHIND THE TARDIS

The magical way that *Doctor Who* is created has inspired countless people in their lives and careers. Many of us have been drawn to the show because of its boundless creativity. From monsters made out of bubble wrap to the genius of modern-day special effects, the creation of worlds, creatures and characters draws us in and propels our imagination.

Many of us may have a keen interest in writing because of *Doctor Who*'s exciting scripts, books and comics. A show that can go anywhere in space and time means there's the opportunity for anybody to create it or write it. With shows like *Doctor Who Confidential* and endless coverage of the making of *Who*, it's no wonder we too want to become a piece of that world.

Some might find that discovering how adventures are created removes the magic of the finished product, but sometimes delving into how an episode is made from script to screen can be the most magical process. We get the truth behind how a world is realised or the run-down of how a monster came to life. The layers of our favourite characters are revealed as we see what shapes them or how their costumes are created. We've even seen a hilarious peek into the reality of a day on set: a Cyberman smoking a cigarette or a dancing Ood!

Whether you're interested in costume, design, marketing, scriptwriting, SFX, make-up or production, *Doctor Who* gives us access to the very best. Producing pioneer

Verity Lambert was the only female drama producer when she began work on *Who* in 1963, and the youngest too, at just twenty-eight years old. Legendary writer Russell T Davies defied the odds to bring the show back to us in 2005. Chris Chibnall gave us our first two female Doctors, who showed us that anyone can be the hero. We've had countless brilliant minds breathe life into the show over the past six decades, giving us a workshop on how to make incredible escapism for people all over the world – and inspire millions to be brilliant.

It's hard to be a fan of *Doctor Who* without immersing yourself in its history. From Television Centre to Roath Lock Studios, *Who* has been created all over the UK (and occasionally abroad) to bring us an entire world of adventures. There's so much to learn, fuelling creative minds everywhere. So, take one last dive into this celebration of *Doctor Who* by quizzing yourself on its behind-the-scenes history. This is the ultimate test, so grab the TARDIS console and get ready for a trip of a lifetime. You never know, it might soon be your turn to create adventures in space and time …

Behind the Blue Box

It was originally thought that the TARDIS would have a fully working chameleon circuit, rather than being stuck as a police box. However, it was quickly realised that it would be too expensive to build a new TARDIS exterior for every story. The ship remained a police box and it was written into lore that the chameleon circuit stopped working while disguised in 1960s London – leaving the Doctor's legendary ship a blue box recognisable across space and time.

1. Which story was producer Verity Lambert's last on *Doctor Who*?

2. Who has written the most individual episodes of *Doctor Who*?

3. Which fake show did Jenna Coleman pretend she was auditioning for, when in fact she was auditioning for *Doctor Who*?

4. In which castle were scenes from 'Silver Nemesis' filmed?

5. Who designed the first ever TARDIS interior?

6. Which story was the first to be filmed in HD?

7. How many arrangements of the *Doctor Who* theme tune did Delia Derbyshire create?

8. Which *Doctor Who* story is recorded as the most watched ever on its original broadcast in the UK?

9. How was the TARDIS dematerialisation sound effect created?

10. Which classic *Doctor Who* story was the last to be filmed before the show was cancelled?

11. Which costume designer worked on Series 1 of New Who?

12. True or False? The first ever episode of *Doctor Who* ('An Unearthly Child', 1963) was filmed twice.

13. Which story had the working title 'Wounded Time'?

14. Which writer is the only person to have written for the classic and new series of *Doctor Who*?

Who's Most Viewed?

Doctor Who's fiftieth anniversary episode, 'The Day of the Doctor' (2013), saw the return of David Tennant as the Tenth Doctor and the introduction of John Hurt as the War Doctor, alongside Matt Smith. Simulcast in 94 countries, it was screened across cinemas and brought in 12.8 million viewers in the UK alone. It may be one of the most-viewed episodes of all time – but the final figures are a mystery due to how widely broadcast it was!

Which *Who* Writer...

Whether you're a serial *Doctor Who* binge watcher or just stick with repeats of a few favourites, you're bound to know the writing of the show inside out.

You'd probably recognise a Moffat twist or a classic Robert Holmes' script from a mile away. Maybe you're more of a New *Who* person and prefer to stick with the showrunners, or perhaps you've memorised every writer of the Classic series. However invested you are in the writers of *Doctor Who*, there's someone we all remember. How about Richard Curtis and his beautiful van Gogh portrayal, or David Whitaker and his legendary Dalek stories?

Find out how much you know and maybe learn about a few writers from across time and space by guessing which *Who* writer...

A) Wrote 'Planet of the Ood'?

B) Put dinosaurs on a spaceship?

C) Wrote the deadly cheetah people?

D) Wrote 'Planet of Giants'?

E) Penned Jon Pertwee's first story?

F) Made Amy Pond wait on a far-away world?

G) Told the story of what happened at Villa Diodati?

H) Wrote the final regular appearance of Tegan Jovanka?

I) Introduced the Doctor and her friends to Rosa Parks?

J) Turned the Doctor human for a while?

K) Threw the Fourth Doctor from a telescope?

L) Wrote 'The Enemy of the World'?

M) Introduced the Rani?

N) Made Rose Tyler befriend a lone Dalek?

O) Wrote the death of Clara Oswald?

What's in a Name?

Some *Who* companions nearly had completely different names to what they ended up being called. Barbara Wright, Susan Foreman and Ian Chesterton were originally going to be called Bridget, Lola and Cliff. Vicki was almost Tanni, Lukki or Millie. Tegan ended up with a surname that was suggested to be her first, becoming Tegan Jovanka, instead of Tegan or Jovanka. It's hard to believe these iconic characters might have been named so differently.

ANSWERS

CHAPTER ONE: THE DOCTOR'S MANY FACES

Q1: B, William Hartnell played the First Doctor, staying in the role for three years.

Q2: B, The Second Doctor loved to play the recorder.

Q3: C, The Doctor was exiled to Earth.

Q4: True, Tom Baker played the Doctor for seven years consecutively.

Q5: A, He wore celery on his jacket lapel.

Q6: B, Colin Baker played the Sixth Doctor.

Q7: C, Ace called the Doctor 'Professor'.

Q8: A, Paul McGann debuted as the Doctor in the 1996 TV movie *Doctor Who*.

Q9: B, Christopher Eccleston played the Doctor for one series in 2005.

Q10: C, The Tenth Doctor continued travelling with Rose Tyler.

Q11: A, Fish fingers and custard was his favourite.

Q12: B, John Hurt played the War Doctor.

Q13: A, The Twelfth Doctor had a Scottish accent.

Q14: B, Jodie Whittaker became the first female Doctor in 2017.

Q15: A, She was named the Fugitive Doctor.

Q16: B, Ncuti Gatwa.

Costume Conundrum

Scarf - Fourth Doctor

Fez - Eleventh Doctor

Converse trainer – Tenth Doctor

Pull-over jumper – Seventh Doctor

Cat pin badge – Sixth Doctor

Leather jacket – Ninth Doctor

CHAPTER TWO: FRIENDS OF THE DOCTOR

Q1: B, The Doctor's grandaughter is named Susan.

Q2: A, Sarah Jane Smith was a journalist.

Q3: B, Amy Pond grew up in Leadworth.

Q4: C, Ace created her own explosive called Nitro-9.

Q5: B, The Doctor and Martha met the Judoon.

Q6: True, Rose travelled with both the Ninth and Tenth Doctors.

Q7: A, Peri Brown travelled with the Fifth and Sixth Doctors.

Q8: C, Clara Oswald worked at Coal Hill, the school the Doctor's grandaughter attended in 1963.

Q9: True, Mel was played by Bonnie Langford.

Q10: C, The Doctor and River got married in 'The Wedding of River Song'.

Q11: C, Jo Grant left the Doctor in 'The Green Death'.

Q12: B, We met two incarnations of Romana on-screen.

Q13: B, Bill's surname was Potts.

Q14: A, the Doctor calls Ryan, Yaz and Graham her 'Fam'.

Q15: C, Wilf was Donna Noble's grandfather.

CHAPTER THREE: THE TARDIS

Q1: B, TARDIS stands for Time and Relative Dimension in Space.

Q2: A, The TARDIS has a broken Chameleon Circuit which means it is stuck as a police box.

Q3: B, The TARDIS is bigger on the inside.

Q4: B, The TARDIS is powered by Artron energy.

Q5: True, The Thirteenth Doctor's TARDIS had a biscuit dispenser.

Q6: C, The Doctor sometimes refers to the TARDIS as sexy.

Q7: A, The TARDIS did not get along with Clara Oswald.

Q8: B, The Doctor stole the TARDIS from Gallifrey.

Q9: C, The TARDIS is occasionally taken to Cardiff Bay to refuel.

Q10: A, The TARDIS is a Type 40.

Q11: True, The TARDIS has a translation circuit for its passengers.

Q12: B, The Ninth and Tenth Doctor's console room.

Q13: C, The human version of the TARDIS was portrayed by Suranne Jones.

Q14: A, The round décor on the walls are referred to as 'the round things'.

Q15: B, The TARDIS has a sign on the front door that says 'Pull to Open'.

Q16: A, River Song knows how to fly the TARDIS even better than the Doctor.

Q17: False – Friends of the Doctor are often given a TARDIS key.

Q18: B, The column in the centre of the TARDIS is called the Time Rotor.

TARDIS Wordsearch

P	A	R	T	R	O	N	E	N	E	R	G	Y	T
N	T	M	O	O	R	O	R	E	Z	R	E	N	T
C	Y	T	L	E	S	R	S	S	Y	O	Y	O	M
O	P	E	Y	O	P	N	I	R	L	M	E	D	I
N	E	N	A	O	T	T	R	E	L	O	O	L	R
S	F	H	O	N	F	E	D	E	N	P	F	T	Y
O	O	E	T	D	I	N	I	R	F	I	H	O	O
L	R	O	N	P	U	I	M	S	S	N	A	O	F
E	T	I	I	O	E	O	T	D	F	S	R	C	T
O	Y	B	R	C	L	N	B	H	O	O	M	S	M
O	T	N	E	M	U	N	O	M	T	S	O	H	G
L	T	H	E	R	I	F	T	R	R	O	N	F	P
R	G	H	E	O	S	E	I	E	T	E	Y	E	Y
O	P	O	L	I	C	E	B	O	X	Y	Y	X	I

CHAPTER FOUR: ALIENS & ADVERSARIES

Q1: C, The Slitheen invaded London in 'Aliens of London/ World War Three'.

Q2: A, The Fourth Doctor was the first Doctor to meet the Zygons in 'Terror of the Zygons' (1975).

Q3: B, You must not blink in the presence of a Weeping Angel, or they will speedily zap you back in time when you aren't looking!

Q4: True, all three Doctors have faced off against the Sea Devils.

Q5: B, The Doctor met the Pting aboard the *Tsuranga*.

Q6: A, Sontar-ha was the Sontarans' battle cry.

Q7: C, Peter Kay portrayed the Abzorbaloff in 'Love & Monsters'.

Q8: B, The Nestene Consciousness controlled plastic shop-window dummies to cause chaos on Earth on multiple occasions.

Q9: A, The Doctor and his friends wrote tally marks on their bodies to remind them how many Silents they had encountered after forgetting them.

Q10: B, The Ice Warriors come from Mars.

Q11: C, The Beast possessed the Ood to murder members of the Sanctuary Base crew during their first *Doctor Who* story.

Q12: False, The Silurians are originally from Earth.

Q13: B, The Nimons resemble Minotaurs.

Q14: A, The Doctor and Donna fought the Racnoss in 'The Runaway Bride'.

Q15: B, The Great Intelligence returned for *Doctor Who's* fiftieth anniversary series.

Monster Madness

Q1: The Ood

Q2: The Silurians

Q3: The Sontarans

Q4: The Silence/A Silent

Q5: Adipose

Q6: Lupari

Q7: Judoon

Q8: The Zarbi

CHAPTER FIVE: DEADLY DALEKS

Q1: C, Terry Nation wrote the first Dalek story and came up with the concept for the Doctor's most feared enemy.

Q2: C, The Daleks come from Skaro.

Q3: A, Davros was the creator of the Daleks.

Q4: B, The Daleks' catchphrase is 'Exterminate!'

Q5: B, Inside a Dalek casing lives a Dalek mutant.

Q6: A, The Kaleds are the race that the Daleks originated from.

Q7: C, The Tenth Doctor met the Daleks in 1930s New York.

Q8: True, Dalek casing is made from Dalekanium.

Q9: B, Dalek Sec has black casing.

Q10: A, Oswin Oswald turned out to be a Dalek, but didn't realise herself to be so.

Q11: C, The Daleks threaten London in 1963 during 'Remembrance of the Daleks'.

Q12: C, There was only one Dalek in 'Resolution' (2019).

Q13: A, The Daleks served tea to Winston Churchill in 'Victory of the Daleks'.

Q14: B, Rose Tyler touched a Dalek, which then absorbed some of her DNA.

Q15: False, Jo Grant met the Daleks on multiple occasions.

Q16: A, The Daleks measure time in 'Rels'.

Q17: B, Dalek ships usually take the form of a saucer.

Scrambled Daleks

Skaro

Exterminate

Plunger

Eyestalk

Davros

Dalek Emperor

Cult of Skaro

Time War

Gunstick

Reality Bomb

Dalek Sec

Dalek Caan

Dalek Mutant

Rels

CHAPTER SIX: HISTORICAL ADVENTURES

Q1: B, The Tenth Doctor married Elizabeth I during 'The Day of the Doctor' (2013).

Q2: The Thirteenth Doctor, Yaz, Ryan and Graham met Rosa Parks on their first trip into the past.

Q3: A, Barbara Wright assumed the identity of Yetexa when the Aztec people mistook her for the ancient God.

Q4: Sarah Jane Smith (accidentally!) travelled with the Third Doctor to the thirteenth century, where they met the Sontarans in 'The Time Warrior' (1973).

Q5: C, Van Gogh dedicated *Vase with Twelve Sunflowers* to Amy after they became firm friends in 'Vincent and the Doctor'.

Q6: A, The First Doctor met Richard the Lionheart in 'The Crusade' (1965).

Q7: B, 'The Eaters of Light' (2017) answered the question of what happened to the Ninth Legion of the Roman army.

Q8: C, The Doctor and Rose were intending to land in Sheffield 1979.

Q9: They met the Lone Cyberman, described by Mary Shelley as a 'Modern Prometheus'.

Q10: A, Clara Oswald had a poster of Marcus Aurelius on her wall when she was a teenager.

Q11: B, The Vespiform resembled a giant Earth wasp.

Q12: Steven Moffat wrote 'The Empty Child/The Doctor Dances' (2005).

Q13: Ada Lovelace helped the Thirteenth Doctor fend off the Master in 'Spyfall' (2020)

Q14: C, The Doctor and H. G. Wells met and adventured during 'Timelash' (1985).

Q15: True! The Doctor and Martha were zapped back in time by the Angels, stuck in 1969.

Q16: The 1814 frost fair was held on the River Thames.

Q17: A, The Doctor first met the Rani in a nineteenth-century village named 'Killingsworth'.

Q18: The Carrionites used their witchy magic on Shakespeare to attempt to free their race and take over the Earth.

History Mystery

Episode	Historical Figure
War of the Sontarans	Mary Seacole
The Unquiet Dead	Charles Dickens
The Girl in the Fireplace	Madame de Pompadour
The Impossible Astronaut/ Day of the Moon	Richard Nixon

The Reign of Terror	Napoleon Bonaparte
Rosa	Martin Luther King
The Haunting of Villa Diodati	Mary Shelley
Nikola Tesla's Night of Terror	Nikola Tesla
The Unicorn and the Wasp	Agatha Christie
Dinosaurs on a Spaceship	Queen Nefertiti

CHAPTER SEVEN: THE MASTER

Q1: We are first introduced to the Master in 'Terror of the Autons' (1971).

Q2: A, The Master allied with the Cheetah People in 'Survival'.

Q3: Missy gave Clara Oswald the Doctor's phone number to force a friendship between the pair so that she could go on to easily manipulate the Doctor.

Q4: A, The Tissue Compression Eliminator is the device that compresses the Master's victims, leaving them as tiny doll-sized corpses.

Q5: C, The Master was found on the planet Tersurus during 'The Deadly Assassin'.

Q6: The Master called himself 'Harold Saxon' when he created a fake identity to become the Prime Minister of the UK.

Q7: B, The Master is offered a new regeneration cycle if he helps the Time Lords rescue the Doctors, who had been taken out of time and dropped into the Death Zone on Gallifrey in 'The Five Doctors'.

Q8: Two incarnations of the Master appeared in 'World Enough and Time/The Doctor Falls' – Missy and the Harold Saxon Master.

Q9: A, The Ninth Doctor did not meet the Master on-screen.

Q10: The Master used the Cybermen and Time Lord corpses to create the 'CyberMaster' race.

Q11: Eric Roberts (brother of Hollywood actress Julia Roberts) played the Master in the 1996 TV movie, *Doctor Who*.

Q12: A, The Master took on the form of Nyssa's father Tremas in the 'The Keeper of Traken' and kept this body until the 1996 *Doctor Who* movie.

Q13: The Master owns a laser screwdriver, which is biometrically secured so that only he can use it.

Q14: B, UNIT captured the Master and imprisoned him off the coast of England, where he then attempted to ally with the Sea Devils and help them take the Earth.

Q15: C, William Hughes was the youngest actor to take on the role of the Master – playing him as a child during 'The Sound of Drums' (2007) and 'The End of Time' (2009).

CHAPTER EIGHT: FUTURE TRAVELS

Q1: The end of the Earth – The Ninth Doctor takes Rose to watch the Sun expand and destroy the Earth.

Q2: A, Dodo infects the Humans and Monoids with a cold when she arrives on a generation starship with the First Doctor and Steven Taylor.

Q3: B, The Star Whale carried *Starship UK* as the ship's mode of transport.

Q4: 'The Caves of Androzani' was the episode in which the Fifth Doctor regenerated.

Q5: C, The Thirteenth Doctor and her friends met the Dregs on Orphan 55.

Q6: Leela became the Fourth Doctor's companion after he met her in the far future, forcing her way onto the TARDIS and becoming his travelling partner in 1977's 'The Face of Evil.'

Q7: True – The Second Doctor and his friends met the Ice Warriors on the Moon in 2089 during 'The Seeds of Death'.

Q8: A, Some of the population of New New York were hidden and kept down in the Motorway so that they wouldn't be infected by the virus.

Q9: C, 'The Daleks' was the first television story that saw *Doctor Who* set in the future.

Q10: B, The Seventh Doctor and Ace travelled to Segonax after being invited to see the Psychic Circus in 'The Greatest Show in the Galaxy'.

Q11: The Twelfth Doctor and Clara Oswald faced off against 'ghosts' in 'Under the Lake'/'Before the Flood'.

Q12: A, The Kandyman appeared to be made out of Liquorice Allsorts.

Q13: Lady Cassandra eventually took over the body of her servant Chip, the form in which she died.

Q14: The Sixth Doctor and Peri Brown went to Varos to look for Zeiton-7 in order to fix the TARDIS.

Q15: B, The Third Doctor and Jo Grant discovered that the Earth had been warring with the Draconians when they landed in the twenth-sixth century during 1973's 'Frontier in Space'

Q16: C, Kerb!am was the retailer that the Thirteenth Doctor and her friends visited – where 'Kerb!am Men' delivered packages to the humans living on Kandoka.

Find the Future

D	E	N	D	O	F	T	H	E	W	O	R	L	D
R	M	E	M	O	J	I	B	O	T	S	R	N	I
A	F	B	S	D	N	A	R	D	O	L	E	F	I
G	M	A	D	N	I	K	E	R	U	T	U	F	O
O	N	M	C	O	E	I	O	L	I	E	A	E	T
N	I	O	I	E	P	D	L	O	E	P	S	I	L
F	E	N	F	R	O	R	U	A	R	E	C	O	H
I	B	O	O	N	B	F	I	E	W	L	L	A	I
R	B	I	D	O	R	A	B	L	I	N	N	A	O
E	O	D	L	E	F	A	I	O	H	M	N	I	S
D	B	S	L	D	N	L	R	R	E	A	T	G	R
K	E	R	B	L	A	M	D	B	F	L	U	R	E
L	I	V	E	F	O	T	E	N	A	L	P	D	T
F	S	N	A	I	N	O	C	A	R	D	W	N	T

CHAPTER NINE: THE CYBERMEN

Q1: B, The Cybermen first debuted in 1966 story 'The Tenth Planet'.

Q2: Gold – Some species of Cybermen are allergic to gold.

Q3: A, Bill Potts was converted into a Cyberman during 'World Enough and Time/The Doctor Falls'.

Q4: True – Dr Kit Pedler and Gerry Davis came up with the idea of the Cybermen.

Q5: A Cyberleader – Black-handled Cybermen are usually ranked as the leader of the bunch!

Q6: C, A tomb of Cybermen was found on Telos.

Q7: Handles – The Doctor affectionately named his Cyber friend 'Handles' during 'The Time of the Doctor' (2013).

Q8: B, The Cybermen have an Emotional Inhibitor that stops them from feeling emotions.

Q9: C, The original Cybermat design was based on wood lice.

Q10: 'Delete!' is the Cybermen's now-famous catchphrase.

Q11: A, The Fourth Doctor battled the Cybermen on Nerva during 'Revenge of the Cybermen' (1975)

Q12: B, We first see the Cybermen fly in the 2014 story 'Dark Water/Death in Heaven'.

Q13: James Corden played Craig Owens, who first appeared as the Doctor's friend in 2010 episode 'The Lodger'

Q14: True – Henry van Statten held a Cyberman helmet/head in his museum, as seen in 'Dalek' (2005).

Q15: A, Ashad chased the Cyberium through time so that he could attempt to re-build the Cyber-Empire.

Cyber Match

Episode	Year
The Next Doctor	2008
Revenge of the Cybermen	1975
Rise of the Cybermen/The Age of Steel	2006
The Tomb of the Cybermen	1967
The Tenth Planet	1966
Nightmare in Silver	2013
Ascension of the Cybermen/The Timeless Children	2020
Attack of the Cybermen	1985
Dark Water/Death in Heaven	2014

CHAPTER TEN: FRIENDS OF THE DOCTOR, PART TWO

Intro Quiz

A: Rose Tyler

B: Adric

C: Amy Pond

D: Susan Foreman

E: Martha Jones

F: Victoria Waterfield

G: Rory Williams

H: Peri Brown

I: Wilfred Mott

J: Jo Grant

K: Bill Potts

Q1: B, Liz Shaw appeared in four Third Doctor stories.

Q2: The trio are nicknamed the Paternoster Gang, due to their residence on Paternoster Row in the City of London.

Q3: A, Professor Marius originally built K9 in the year 5000.

Q4: C, Ian and Barbara returned back to London via a Dalek time ship, two years after they left their home.

Q5: Clara Oswald told the First Doctor which TARDIS to steal after jumping into the Doctor's time stream and splintering off into millions of versions of herself throughout history.

Q6: Zoe Heriot and Jamie McCrimmon had their minds wiped of their travels with the Doctor and were sent back to their own time with only their first encounter with their friend left in their minds.

Q7: B, Osgood's first name is Petronella.

Q8: A, Ben and Polly faced off against the Chameleons in their final adventure with the Doctor.

Q9: Matt Lucas played Twelfth Doctor companion Nardole, first appearing in 'The Husbands of River Song' (2015).

Q10: B, The Brigadier first appeared in 'The Web of Fear' (1968), where we first meet him as a colonel, before he had been promoted to his famed status as the Brigadier.

Q11: Mickey Smith stayed behind in a parallel universe, believing there was more for him in a world where his gran was still alive.

Q12: A, Nyssa originally came from the planet Traken, where she met the Fourth Doctor.

Q13: True! Harry was never seen on-screen inside the TARDIS, despite appearing in seven stories.

Q14: Grace accidentally caused the Seventh Doctor's regeneration while attempting to perform surgery on him after he was shot by a gang outside his TARDIS.

Q15: B, The Mara possessed Tegan Jovanka during 'Snakedance' (1983).

Who Almost Made It?

Q1: Joan Redfern

Q2: Perkins

Q3: Astrid Peth

Q4: Ada Lovelace

Q5: Journey Blue

Q6: Rita

Q7: Lynda Moss

CHAPTER 11: EARTH INVASIONS

Q1: The Saturnyns ended up on Earth during 'The Vampires of Venice' (2010), after losing their planet and falling through a crack in time. They intended to flood Venice and use kidnapped women to procreate and save their race.

Q2: The Cybermen attempted to control the human race via a signal from International Electromatics devices in 'The Invasion' (1968).

Q3: When the Sontarans invaded Earth in 'War of the Sontarans' (2021), Russia and China were renamed throughout history as 'Sontar' – after their home planet.

Q4: In 1975's 'Terror of the Zygons', the Zygons used the Skarasen in their attempt to take over Earth – a creature from their home world which they cybernetically enhanced and fashioned into a weapon, which was mistaken for being the Loch Ness Monster!

Q5: The Sycorax found and followed Earth space probe 'Guinevere One', using the blood samples included to control a portion of the population and attempt to take the Earth, during 'The Christmas Invasion' (2005).

Q6: A Rutan came to be on Earth in 1902 in 'Horror of Fang Rock' (1977), when its ship crash-landed into the sea – it then planned to turn the Earth into a base to launch an attack on the Rutan's sworn enemy, the Sontarans.

Q7: Cybermen who took the form of ghosts began appearing on Earth for two months before the Doctor and Rose landed back in London and discovered the mystery in 'Army of Ghosts/Doomsday' (2006).

Q8: The Daleks were drilling to the centre of the Earth to remove the core and replace it with a system that would mean they could pilot our planet like a ship ('The Dalek Invasion of Earth', 1964).

Q9: The bodies of the Slitheen are calcium-based.

Q10: During 'The Android Invasion' (1975) the Kraals planned to wipe out the people of Earth with a deadly virus spread around our planet via their androids.

Q11: The Nestene Consciousness attempted to invade the Earth three times – twice thwarted by the Third Doctor ('Spearhead from Space', 1970, and 'Terror of the Autons', 1971), and then stopped by the Ninth Doctor and Rose Tyler in 'Rose' (2005).

Q12: The Boneless come from a two-dimensional universe and were able to change 3D-objects into 2D-objects in our universe ('Flatline', 2014).

Q13: A, The Doctor, Jamie and Victoria landed in Covent Garden station before discovering the Yeti were haunting the London Underground in 'The Web of Fear' (1968).

Q14: The Monks used a virtually simulated reality of planet Earth to plan an invasion and take control of the human race in 'Extremis' (2017).

Q15: The Eleventh Doctor, Amy and Rory Pond experience the 'Year of the Slow Invasion' during the 2012 episode 'The Power of Three', when millions of tiny black cubes appeared overnight on Earth, residing there for a year before beginning to kill the human race.

Name that Invasion!

Question	Clue	Answer
1	Snow. Gas. Wales. Author.	The Unquiet Dead (2005)
2	Moon. Rocket. Solar. Ice.	The Seeds of Death (1969)
3	Silver. Royal. Comet. Cyber.	Silver Nemesis (1988)
4	Chips. School. Oil.	School Reunion (2006)
5	Plastic Dummies. Exile. Regeneration.	Spearhead from Space (1970)
6	Painting. Trafalgar Square. No More.	The Day of the Doctor (2013)

7	Simulation. Control. Monk.	Extremis (2017)
8	Scotland. Oil. Duplicate.	Terror of the Zygons (1975)
9	Downing Street. Big Ben. Pig.	Aliens of London/ World War Three (2005)
10	Crash-landing. Middle Ages. Warrior.	The Time Warrior (1973)

CHAPTER 12: PLANETS & WORLDS

Q1: The twin planet of Clom (home to the Abzorbaloff) is Raxacoricofallapatorius – from where the Slitheen family originated in 2006's 'Love & Monsters'.

Q2: The Doctor and Jo Grant befriended an Aggedor on Peladon during 'The Curse of Peladon' (1972), who were thought to be extinct, although some still resided in the mountains of the planet.

Q3: Daleks are sent to the Dalek Asylum when they malfunction or go insane, as seen in 'Asylum of the Daleks' (2012).

Q4: The First Doctor first met his friend Vicki on the planet Dido, where her ship had crash-landed, during 'The Rescue' (1965).

Q5: B, The Thirteenth Doctor and her friends got caught up in the Rally of the Twelve Galaxies, when they accidentally ended up on the planet Desolation in 'The Ghost Monument' (2018).

Q6: The Eye of Horus was kept in a pyramid on Mars, sending a signal to Earth that kept 'destroyer of all things' Sutekh imprisoned during 'Pyramids of Mars' (1975).

Q7: A night lasts for twenty-four years on the planet Darillium, where the Twelfth Doctor and River Song share their final date in 'The Husbands of River Song' (2015).

Q8: B, Gallifrey, Draconia, Sontar and Earth all reside in the same Galaxy, named 'Mutter's Spiral' by the Time Lords.

Q9: Davros and the Daleks stole Woman Wept during 'The Stolen Earth/Journey's End' (2008) and placed it in the Medusa Cascade as part of their plan to set off a reality bomb and destroy all of time and space.

Q10: Turlough was exiled from Trion as a political prisoner following a Civil War on his planet ('Planet of Fire' 1984).

Q11: The Ood Sphere and Sense Sphere were both located in the Horsehead Nebula.

Q12: C, Cheetah Planet, home to the Cheetah People and Kitlings, was sentient – visited by the Doctor and Ace in 'Survival' (1989).

Q13: The Church of the Papal Mainframe, led by Tasha Lem, tried to ensure that Trenzalore would be kept safe and stop the Time Lords returning through a crack in time, as they did not want another Time War ('The Time of the Doctor', 2013).

Q14: Telos was home to the Cryons before the Cybermen colonised and murdered most of their race.

Q15: Krop Tor translates as 'The Bitter Pill', originating from a legend that a black hole swallowed and spat out the planet because it was 'poison' ('The Impossible Planet/The Satan Pit', 2006).

Q16: A, There's a deadly lake of mutations from genetic experiments on Skaro, which killed three Thals during 'The Daleks' (1963) while on an expedition to the centre of the Dalek City.

Q17: Vortis is also known as 'The Web Planet', where the First Doctor, Barbara, Ian and Vicki landed and met the Menoptera and the Zarbi in the 1965 story of the same name.

Which World?

Q1: Skaro

Q2: Sto

Q3: Malcassairo

Q4: Alzarius

Q5: Sense Sphere

Q6: Tivoli

Q7: Tythonus

Q8: Time

Q9: Drahva

Q10: Thijar

CHAPTER 13: DEFENDERS OF THE EARTH

Q1: The Brigadier and his daughter Kate Stewart have met eleven incarnations of the Doctor (including the War Doctor) on screen – with the Sixth, Eighth, Ninth and Fugitive Doctors being the only incarnations that haven't met either Stewart.

Q2: The Torchwood Institute was founded in 1879 by Queen Victoria, after meeting the Tenth Doctor and Rose Tyler in 'Tooth and Claw' (2006) and deciding the United Kingdom needed to be protected from alien threat.

Q3: The Bane called Luke the 'Archetype' – who was created in an attempt to find a way to get the two per cent of the population who wouldn't drink 'Bubble Shock!' to change their minds. He was awoken and found by Maria Jackson and later adopted by Sarah Jane Smith ('Invasion of the Bane', *The Sarah Jane Adventures*, 2007).

Q4: The tear in space and time around Coal Hill School was created by an excess of Artron Energy in the area, created by the TARDIS landing there so often. Creatures from other worlds were attracted to the tear in space and thus the Coal Hill defenders were born to protect the school from threat.

Q5: The Master, disguised as Harold Saxon, sent members of Torchwood Three on a wild goose chase to the Himalayas so that they wouldn't be present to help Captain Jack, Martha Jones and the Doctor in stopping his plan ('The Sound of Drums', 2007).

Q6: The Blue Box Files podcast – run by Cleo Proctor, Shawna Thompson and Abby McPhail – aimed to uncover the mystery of the 'Blue Box' and the mysterious Doctor associated with it, in 2022's *Doctor Who: Redacted*.

Q7: Two members of the Slitheen-Blathereen family gifted Sarah Jane Smith some deadly Rakweed ('The Gift', *The Sarah Jane Adventures*, 2009).

Q8: Torchwood Two was based in Glasgow, Scotland ('Everything Changes', *Torchwood*, 2006).

Q9: Cleo Proctor was saved by the Tenth Doctor, but lost her father during the 'Red Hatching' in 2008, where giant red eggs sprang up all over Earth, hatching terrifying creatures ('Salvation', *Doctor Who: Redacted* 2022).

Q10: Charlie Smith was actually an alien prince from the planet Rhodia. He was the last of the Rhodians – rescued by the Twelfth Doctor from a war on his planet and taken to Coal Hill School to live as a teenager.

Q11: During 'Survivors of the Flux' (2021), it was described that UNIT had missed the incident at 'Post Office Tower'. This was one of the reasons why Alistair Lethbridge-Stewart was brought into UNIT, because War Machines – invented

by super computer WOTAN – attempted to take over
London in 1966.

Q12: *Torchwood* member Toshiko Sato was sent to London
in 2006 to investigate a Space Pig that had crash-landed
into Big Ben – this turned out to be a decoy, planted by the
Slitheen ('Aliens of London', 2005).

Q13: Everybody turned against Clyde Langer in 'The Curse
of Clyde Langer' (*The Sarah Jane Adventures*, 2011), after
he touched an ancient totem pole that left him 'cursed'.

Q14: April MacLean shared a heart with Corakinus after
he came to Coal Hill School looking for Charlie Smith. April
fired a displacement gun at the Shadow King, scattering his
heart across the universe and leaving the pair sharing April's
heart ('For Tonight We Might Die', *Class*, 2016).

Q15: Winifred Bambera held the rank of Brigadier at UNIT
in the late nineties, when the Seventh Doctor and Ace met
her during 'Battlefield' (1989).

Q16: Martha Jones travelled with the Doctor and went on
to work with both UNIT and Torchwood.

The Black Archive: Memory Mayhem

   A)   ~~For Tonight~~ We Might Die

   B)   The ~~Green~~ Death

   C)   ~~Dead~~ Man Walking

D)   Whatever Happened ~~to Sarah Jane?~~

E)   Invasion of the ~~Dinosaurs~~

F)   The ~~Metaphysical Engine,~~ or What Quill Did

G)   ~~Exit~~ Wounds

H)   Mona Lisa's ~~Revenge~~

I)   The Power of ~~Three~~

J)   ~~Eye~~ of the Gorgon

K)   Redacted: ~~Salvation~~

L)   ~~Turn~~ Left

M)   Secrets ~~of the Stars~~

N)   They Keep Killing ~~Suzie~~

O)   ~~Brave-ish Heart~~

CHAPTER 14: GALLIFREY & THE TIME LORDS

Q1: Gallifrey resides in the constellation of Kasterborous.

Q2: The Death Zone was used in the Game of Rassilon – as seen in 'The Five Doctors' (1983), where five incarnations of the Doctor and their companions were taken out of time and dropped on Gallifrey to partake in the game.

Q3: The Eighth Doctor regenerated into the War Doctor after dying in a spaceship crash on the planet Karn, where the Sisterhood of Karn gave him an elixir to trigger his regeneration. This meant that he could choose traits for his new body that would serve him in his mission to become a Time War warrior ('The Night of the Doctor', 2013).

Q4: The indigenous people of Gallifrey were called the Shobogans, who eventually became the Time Lords after Tecteun spliced them with the Doctor's DNA and gave them the ability to regenerate ('The Timeless Children', 2020).

Q5: The Hand of Omega transformed stars into supernovas in order to fuel time travel for the people of Gallifrey.

Q6: The Doctor was found as a child at a boundary to another dimension by Tecteun, who took them in and experimented on them.

Q7: The Time Lords grant the Doctor a new regeneration cycle in 'The Time of the Doctor' (2013).

Q8: Timothy Dalton portrayed Rassilon in the Tenth Doctor's regeneration story, 'The End of Time' (2009).

Q9: Gallifrey first appeared in 1969's 'The War Games', during the trial of the Second Doctor.

Q10: A Time Lord mind is uploaded to the Matrix when it dies – an electrical scan is made at the moment of death and transferred, as described in 'The Deadly Assassin' (1976).

Q11: Cloister Bells could be found inside the TARDIS and on Gallifrey, and usually signified great danger.

Q12: The Doctor was exiled to Earth for violating the Time Lord's non-interference policy in 'The War Games' (1969).

Q13: The Vardans invaded and broke down Gallifrey's defences, then allowed the Sontarans to attack, in 1978's 'The Invasion of Time'.

Q14: The Monk was the first Time Lord to appear in the show aside from the Doctor and Susan Foreman, who appeared in 'The Time Meddler' (1965).

Q15: The Capitol resided on the continent of Wild Endeavour.

The Crossword of Rassilon

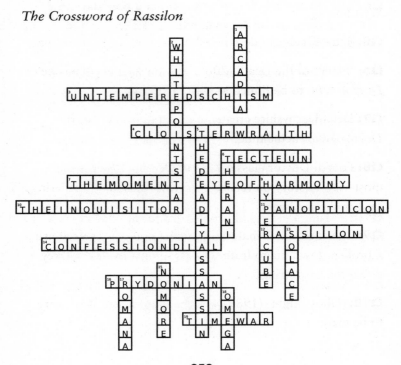

CHAPTER 15: BEHIND THE TARDIS

Q1: 'Mission to the Unknown' (1965) was producer Verity Lambert's final *Doctor Who* story.

Q2: Robert Holmes has written the most single *Doctor Who* episodes, clocking up a total of sixty-four.

Q3: Jenna Coleman had to pretend she was auditioning for 'Men on Waves' while auditioning for *Doctor Who*, which is an anagram of 'Woman 7', as she was the Doctor's companion for the seventh series.

Q4: 'Silver Nemesis' (1988) was filmed at Arundel Castle in West Sussex.

Q5: Peter Brachacki designed the first ever TARDIS console.

Q6: 'Planet of the Dead' (2009) was the first ever episode of *Doctor Who* to be filmed in high definition.

Q7: Delia Derbyshire created four arrangements of the *Doctor Who* theme tune.

Q8: Fourth Doctor classic 'City of Death' (1979) is the most-viewed story on record ever, with Episode 4 garnering 16.1 million viewers.

Q9: The TARDIS dematerialisation sound was created using a broken-down piano frame, by scraping a front-door key down the bass string!

Q10: 'Ghost Light' (1989) was the final classic *Who* story to be made.

Q11: Lucinda Wright was the costume designer for Series 1 of the new series of *Doctor Who* (2005).

Q12: True. Two versions of 'An Unearthly Child' (1963) were filmed. The story had to be shot again because *Who* creator and producer Sydney Newman felt that the characterisation of the Doctor was not correct and there were also a number of production errors in the episode.

Q13: 2005 episode 'Father's Day', by Paul Cornell, had the working title of 'Wounded Time'.

Q14: Rona Munro is the only person who has written for classic and new *Who*, with 1989's 'Survival' and 2017's 'The Eaters of Light'.

Which Who *Writer...*

A)   Keith Temple ('Planet of the Ood', 2008).

B)   Chris Chibnall ('Dinosaurs on a Spaceship', 2012).

C)   Rona Munro ('Survival', 1989).

D)   Louis Marks ('Planet of Giants', 1964).

E)   Robert Holmes ('Spearhead from Space', 1970).

F)   Tom MacRae ('The Girl Who Waited', 2011).

G)   Maxine Alderton ('The Haunting of Villa Diodati', 2020).

H)   Eric Saward ('Resurrection of the Daleks', 1984).

I)   Malorie Blackman and Chris Chibnall ('Rosa', 2018).

J)   Paul Cornell, Vinay Patel and Chris Chibnall ('Human Nature', 2007; 'Fugitive of the Judoon' 2020).

K)   Christopher H. Bidmead ('Logopolis', 1981).

L)   David Whitaker ('The Enemy of the World', 1967).

M)   Pip and Jane Baker ('The Mark of the Rani', 1985).

N)   Robert Shearman ('Dalek', 2005).

O)   Sarah Dollard ('Face the Raven', 2015).

ACKNOWLEDGEMENTS

It may seem a little excessive to want to thank so many people for this little book, however, I cannot express how much gratitude I have for getting to be the author of it. I have wanted to write a *Doctor Who* book ever since I was a small child who escaped into the TARDIS through pages and pages of adventures. So, thank you to Beth Eynon for offering me the opportunity to make my dreams come true by asking me to be the author of this book. I'll be forever thankful that you found me and gave me this chance. I'd like to thank everyone at Bonnier Books UK for being so brilliantly supportive throughout the creation of this celebration of our favourite Time Lord, especially Ciara Lloyd, whose help throughout the editing process has been invaluable.

To Connor Johnston, thank you for pouring over every page and helping me to realise my voice. Your support has helped me to shape this book into the adventure I wanted it to be and I will always be grateful for you. Thank you to Kezia Newson, Gabby De Matteis and Jenny Lippmann for always believing in me – your confidence in my abilities over the years brought me here. Thanks to Josh Whipps for checking every episode title, because apparently we've been saying lots of them wrong our entire lives! Luke Spillane, thank you for answering my random questions when I needed you. Imogen Newman, thank you for your excitement and support, and for being a creative partner that helped me to enjoy my voice in a way I hadn't before this year – you're the best pal and partner a person could ask for!

I cannot write an acknowledgements page in a *Doctor Who* quiz book without mentioning Mikey Snooze and Ioan Morris, who warmly invited me in to host the Quiz of Rassilon almost five years ago, where I learnt many a *Doctor Who* question and answer. Thank you both for being brilliant friends and quiz partners.

To Cameron McEwan, Simon Guerrier and Toby Hadoke – thank you for supporting me when others didn't, and for helping me take steps in my writing career that no doubt led me here.

I'd like to thank my Mum, Jackie Axford, who could have listened when other people told her that a young girl shouldn't like 'a boy's show' such as *Doctor Who*, but let me enjoy it anyway. Finally, I'd like to thank my Aunt Mary, who fuelled my imagination with *Who* books and always supported my passions – I'm sure, if you were still with us, that you would have loved that I got to write my very own *Doctor Who* book.